Easy Beaded Jewelry

Susan Ray and Sue Wilke

"The best and most beautiful things in the world cannot be seen or touched. They must be felt with the heart."

~Helen Keller

An imprint of F+W Publications, Inc.

700 East State Street • Iola, WI 54990-0001
715-445-2214 • 888-457-2873

Library of Congress Catalog Number: 2004093892
ISBN: 0-87349-895-X

Edited by Maria L. Turner
Designed by Marilyn McGrane
Printed in the United States of America

MILAN
gigante
4¢

Dedication

I dedicate this book to all my very best friends, who have been unflinching lifelong companions. They have inspired me, many offering encouragement and lending a hand in times of need: always with a smile and always happy to partner in my next great adventure. There are so many friends that I dare to name them for fear I would have forgotten one or two along the way. In my heart, there is joyful thanks for each and every one of them. Kevin, I thank you for your love, creative inspiration and patience. And thanks to my son, Eric, for delighting in our every move. There are memories made and times remembered. Mostly, there is love.

—Susan Ray

I would like to dedicate this book to:
- My parents, Tom and Mary Jo; thank you for always believing in me.
- My family and friends; you have been such a support for me always.
- The new friends and colleagues I have made through my ever-widening ventures; you have inspired me and fed my creativity.
- Susan Ray, my dear friend, who is always thinking of possibilities and making them happen for everyone she knows. Thank you for this wonderful opportunity and most importantly, your enduring friendship.

—Sue Wilke

Acknowledgments

We are so grateful to so many who helped make this book a reality. Our thanks to:
- KP Books and its parent company, F+W Publications, for again believing.
- Julie Stephani, acquisitions editor, for making this all possible.
- Maria Turner, our ever-thorough and thoroughly wonderful editor.
- Jon Stein for his precise illustrations.
- Bob Best for his beautiful photographs.
- Marilyn McGrane, our graphic design manager, for her honest, open talents.
- Juli Ikonomopoulos for her unwavering commitment to make our ramblings understandable and brief. Juli, we can never thank you enough for setting what spilled from our hearts into such discerning text. We are forever grateful.
- The talented lampwork artists who once again gave so graciously of the work: Deb Roesly, Gary Haun, Tamara Knight, Jill Shank, Roberta Ogborn, Iris Buchholtz, Karen Leonardo, Amy Caswell, Dave and Rebecca Jurgens, Leigh Funk, and Trent and Shawn Warden.
- The amazing talents of the jewelry designers and contributors who filled these pages with magical projects: Susan Brusch, Carol Coyle, Alison Leahy, Christen Stretch, Leigh Meyer, Krysti Kehl, Sandra Raymond, Jessica Italia, Jan Harris, Shannon Williams, Annie Hinton, Darien Kaiser, Linda Zsevc, Brittany Berndtson, Sol Hernandez, and all of the Duhme ladies (Linda, Brenda, Jill, Elisabeth, Laureen, Amber, Loralee, Kelly, Amber, Julie and Linda Duhme Olson).
- Claire Russ without who's smile we could not bead another day and her patience to make such scrumptious amulet bags and earrings.
- Wendy Mullane and Jeanne Holland for "passing the wealth" and allowing us to have the opportunity to present their "secret recipes" for stunning Victorian necklaces, earrings and bracelets.
- Mary Beth Sprengelmeyer for the countless Sundays enjoying each other's company and beading well into the wee hours of the morning.
- Cliff and Barbara Wallach at Halcraft for generously sharing so many wonderful beads used throughout this book.
- FPC, Westrim, Blue Moon, Gutermann, and Judikins for their input and product.

Table of Contents

Introduction

Jewelry plays a special part in our lives. What is your favorite piece of jewelry? Where did it come from? Who gave it to you or made it for you? Can you remember the event? Each piece of jewelry has a story to tell. Like a great memoir of your life, each has sentimental value. It has its own ambiance, its own style. Jewelry helps us relive our times and creates feelings within that somehow say, "Look, I'm special."

Wouldn't it be wonderful to be able to create beaded jewelry just like the pros? How fun would it be to give or wear a piece of jewelry you made and receive the admiration of your friends and family? Beaded jewelry has become a much-loved gift for family and friends. It says, "I made this for you, by my hand."

Today's fashions make beaded jewelry highly sought-after. You will see it on the stars in Hollywood, in the elite mail-order catalogs and even in the best boutiques. How does a designer come up with the ideas to create such wonderful pieces?

Designers take their inspirational cues from everywhere: the world around them, nature, fashion and home decor. They collect ideas from the materials and the beads themselves.

Imagine the possibilities! This book will happily encourage you to let your imagination soar. We will help you create the most stunning beaded jewelry with ease. Mindful that beginners/intermediates need "a little less talk and a lot more action," the book provides the simplest instructions—not too serious, fun and extremely easy-to-follow. We have even created charts helpful for designing and information on tools, components, bead sizes and finishes. We've included some of today's best resources and a personal look at the designers (from all walks of life) who worked so diligently to create the projects within. These artists and designers, with a gift of imagination and the talents of creativity, have placed heart and soul into their work. The beautiful projects within tell their stories.

Whether you are a homemaker or professional woman, wearer or gift giver, heirloom jewelry collector, "wearable art" enthusiast, an embellisher with a penchant towards collage and altered books, crafter or a fine artist, there is something for everyone. We know beaded "art wear" is truly the art and soul of the maker.

Just follow our lead. We know everyone learns best through "play." We have tried to make the text a personal one-on-one. The tips, tricks and designers' secrets take the guesswork out of any project. The book is packed with the best contemporary beaded jewelry, easy step-by-steps to follow and a behind-the-scenes look at the decisions necessary to mastering the art of stringing, even if you are a novice. All of the methodology is strung throughout as a journey of themes. Rather than textbook style, the lessons learned are taught through a series of simple tips that you will find on every page. Most projects can be finished in just one afternoon, and several can be completed in just one hour—just right for the busy crafters of today.

Start with an idea, reflect on your personal style and personality, and then choose a color palette that is right for you. You will create a personal style through understanding design, style, color, texture and opacity, following our "pattern-by-number" approach, you can personalize any project to your own taste and make the most sought-after beaded jewelry with ease.

How will you source your beads? We will teach you to look to your local craft stores or bead shops for beading supplies. You can even transform some thrift shop finds to turn inexpensive beads into tomorrow's heirloom treasures. Acquire vintage components and beads through eBay and other online resources. Create a contemporary art piece, or mix-up various coins and beads from around the world. Get expert advice, design planning, construction, and reclamation ideas.

Each piece of jewelry is individual. Each artist is, too. Create your own "personal jewelry style." Share, laugh and love making one-of-a-kind jewelry for yourself to wear or as gifts for family and friends. The narrative hopes to take the difficulty out of choosing the right beads for any project, as well as providing resources to assist and encourage you. These time-tested techniques will inspire and enlighten you to create jewelry at fractions of the boutique prices.

Find the designer within. You've looked at the latest jewelry designs in an article in your favorite fashion magazine and you say to yourself, "I can do that!" You're absolutely right, you can!

How to Use this Book

Easy Beaded Jewelry is a treasure trove of information and beautiful designs that will prove to be a useful tool and valuable resource on your shelf. We have spent much time and effort to include basic material to get the beginner started off right, thoughtful tips and information of interest to beaders of all skill levels, and a great variety of luscious jewelry designs that provide something for everyone.

Our goals were two-fold. One was to give you as much information and as many designs as possible, and the second goal was to organize it in a straightforward way that is simple and easy to follow. To do this, the book is organized in two parts.

The first part of the book is called "Bead Basics," where you will find everything you need to know to get started. This section covers everything from step-by-steps of basic stringing to the basic supplies you will need and where to find them. We'll even help you identify your personal style. After you have read through the basics, you will have a sound understanding of the techniques needed to do all the projects shown in this book.

The second part of the book features countless jewelry designs that you can make or use as inspiration to develop your own style. The designs progress in the book from simple and casual to more formal and complex, so as you work your way through the book, you will practice the skills you need and gain the confidence necessary to create the jewelry you desire.

Each design includes information you will find valuable, including:

+ a description and beautiful photos of the project
+ what you need (your beads, other supplies and toolbox)
+ where you are most likely to find them
+ approximate time to complete
+ level of expense for the project shown
+ what you need to know (additional skills needed for that project)

There are unique features of this book that are sure to keep you coming back to reference it again and again.

The first is that on *every* project page in the book you will find valuable tips and information. Co-author Susan Ray, owner of Bubbles, Bangles, and Beads in Galena, Ill., has held countless classes teaching thousands of people how to make beaded jewelry in the past three years. The how-to instructions are a distillation of her time-tested techniques, but even more exciting is the multitude of tips, tricks and information she has accumulated.

You'll find this book a great resource tool. Leader lines, as shown in the example at the right, help highlight particular features and findings and also identify specific beads directly on the photographs of the jewelry. This should help you to quickly become familiar with the components and identify what you need or want to include in your own designs.

light green jade round

aventurine chip

malachite round

African jasper round

fossil round

ivory round

howlite round

green jade oval

Regular Cinnamon Latte Bracelet

What a yummy way to have cinnamon latte that lasts and lasts. That's what we call jewelry perks!

Designer: *Susan Ray*

Finished Size: 6¼" without clasp
Where to Get It: Specialty bead shops or catalogs; on the Web
Time to Complete: One weekend
How Much Will It Cost?
A manicure ($20 to $50)

What You Need
5 black-and-tan 10mm
  irregular lampwork rounds
4 tiger-eye 8mm rounds
2 amber 11mm x 10mm
  cathedrals
2 hematite 7mm x 9mm
  rondelle discs
2 Bali sterling silver
  9mm x 2mm spacers*
2 Bali sterling silver
  6mm x 6mm bicones
2 antique silver 8mm bell caps
2 antique sterling silver
  7mm x 8mm bicones
4 sterling silver 3mm rounds
2 sterling silver 2mm x 3mm
  crimp beads
Antique silver clasp set
12" flexible wire
*Available through Fire Mountain Gems

Toolbox
Wire cutters
Flat nose or chain nose pliers
Needle nose pliers

What You Need to Know
See the instructions and information outlined in Single-Strand Basics, pages 23-29.

Tip
● Be sure to avoid using beads that are too large near the sides of your wrist. As with necklaces, consider where on the wrist each bead will lay.

Novice beaders may want to begin by duplicating the jewelry designs exactly as they appear in this book. As you become more comfortable with the basic skills (depending on preference and what is available), you will learn to substitute beads and alternate color schemes.

We offer a photographic image of the designs, marked with leader lines that identify various beads, to guide you in your stringing. Bracelets are shown entirely. When showing necklaces, we have shown half (from the center out) including the clasp, where possible. Have fun with this. Experiment with different bead combinations. The sky's the limit!

We know *Easy Beaded Jewelry* will be a fun book for you to use as you begin making and designing your own beaded jewelry, and we hope it will be a valuable reference for you for years to come.

Tip
● For all the projects in this book, we list a finished length. To be consistent and help you with your designing, the finished lengths for necklaces and bracelets are listed without the clasp. The finished length on earrings is for the dangle only, without the ear wire. Sizes of clasps and ear wires vary greatly. This makes it very easy to adjust the designs using the clasp or findings of your choice.

You may be comfortable and casual or prefer earthy and understated.

You are intrigued and excited by the possibilities in designing and making jewelry, but are hesitant about where to start. What do you do first? Do you shop for beads and tools, or choose a design? The possibilities are exciting and eye-opening; however, they can also be intimidating. Start by taking a moment to reflect on your own personal style, which can be any one of many different choices. Your style may be professional and polished or classic and elegant. You may be comfortable and casual or prefer earthy and understated. Friends may describe you as contemporary with artistic flair. Fun and flamboyant, you may gravitate toward bright and whimsical pieces. You appreciate the soft delicate finer things and can envision yourself in a romantic Victorian setting. Chances are, you may not fit into just one category and your choice of style may be dictated by a special event or your mood. Most of us tend to be a little more complex and appreciate variety as the spice of life.

Personal Style

Narrowing Your Search

Many people are a true mix of styles and claim to be eclectic. Creative and artistic types love that description because whether referring to choices in home furnishings, clothes, food, music or jewelry, it allows the freedom to keep your options open and the license to combine things in fresh new ways that may not be readily apparent if you are loyal to only one theme.

The downside to truly eclectic style is that with all your options open, you are naturally inclusive rather than selective.

If you don't know where to start making jewelry choices, begin by shopping. Go window or idea shopping, first for jewelry styles and then for beads.

When looking for style, get inspiration everywhere. Start by looking at ready-made jewelry designs, such as those in this book. Look in magazines, catalogs, boutiques and department stores. You'll first notice what is the current fashion, but looking more will reveal what styles you consistently gravitate towards. Save that style in your mind and also keep a journal. Be selective and choose only what you have an affinity for. Clip those magazine photos. Sketch out designs. The more ideas you collect that are truly appealing to you, the more clearly you will see your style developing. The designs you collect and save do not necessarily need to be those you want to duplicate. They should be in a style that speaks to you. Maybe only part of a piece of jewelry gives you an idea, like a certain closure or dangle you will want to remember. Now you have begun your own personal idea and style file.

Defining Your Style

Your sense of style—whether casual or formal, bold or subtle, simple or complicated—will reveal to you what types of designs in beaded jewelry will suit you best. For example, if you are tailored and classic, a pattern that will appeal to you is symmetrical with even repeats of beads and possibly a center focal bead or pendant.

Your clothing will also help you make design choices. If you usually wear business attire, such as a jacket with a blouse underneath, that symmetrical design would work well as a choker or in an 18" necklace. If instead you wear a shirt collar and want to have the necklace hang outside, a longer length would be more appropriate.

Most styles can be generalized into two main categories: casual or formal. You may be consistently one or the other, but everyone can be a combination of both. If you are a back-to-the-earth type or an at-home mom, then you may dress primarily casual, but may also be attracted to formal or even frilly when a special occasion arises.

Patterns can be divided into two categories: symmetrical and asymmetrical. Generally, formal designs tend to be a more symmetrical layout. Traditionally, you may find a center pendant or focal evenly balanced between the repeat of beads, graduated in size from large to small, front to back in the piece of jewelry. Asymmetry can add to a casual feel. There is balance in the piece, but the balance is not achieved by evenly mirroring the design.

Of course, there are crossovers, some casual designs can be symmetrical and some formal designs may be asymmetrical. For example, at a formal event you may see someone in a symmetrical graduated strand of pearls and also someone wearing a necklace of randomly strung stone chips, crystals, and vintage beads. Both are dressed appropriately formal; however, the symmetrical necklace is more traditional. Symmetrical placement of elements in your design can skew more formal, while asymmetry can appear to be more casual. Understanding the subtle differences will help you tailor your designs.

Letting "You" Shine Through

When designing a piece of jewelry in a certain style, whether for yourself or for a friend, another consideration is size. Will the size of the beads look appropriate on the person you are designing it for? A fine, lightweight strand of seed beads with a few crystals may be perfect on a young girl or maybe even a bridesmaid, but would be lost on a larger woman. Conversely, lampwork come in all sizes, but may, by the time a set is strung together into a piece of jewelry, be too bold for a young girl or a petite woman.

It's not just the physical size. How about the personality? Large, bold jewelry definitely says "look at me" louder than a simple, tailored piece. You have seen women with multifaceted personalities. The style a woman displays—through her clothes, purses, shoes, and yes, jewelry—tells a lot, even before she opens her mouth. Do you know someone who is always creative, bright and flamboyant? Doesn't it just seem right that she wear bold, whimsical jewelry?

There is so much designing to do, so much jewelry to make—let's get started!

Creativity comes in all styles.

Choosing Your Favorite Colors

Color: Everyone has a favorite color or colors. When you start shopping for beads you will naturally gravitate toward your favorites. Color palettes can reveal styles—earth tones, pastels, brights. What color palettes do you mostly wear?

Not only will you choose beads in your favorite colors, but they will also tend to blend with the colors already in your closet. Some of your first jewelry designs may be something to match an outfit you already have. A long, double-strand necklace may be the perfect answer to go with that chartreuse-and-navy jacket dress you just had to have. Designing jewelry to go with your wardrobe is greatly satisfying.

The longer you make jewelry, especially as you start designing with art glass and lampwork beads, you will also realize that you are shopping for clothes to go with your jewelry. Do you suppose that's how the little black dress got created? What a great background for any designer jewelry.

Color is an important consideration when determining your personal style. Chances are that if you make a piece that goes with something already in your closet, you will love that piece of jewelry just as much as you love the clothing.

When you become interested in beads, you will find them everywhere.

Finding and Storing Your Bead Stock

The most obvious place to start looking for your beads is at large art supply, craft and sewing stores. They will carry a wide selection, including some craft-quality and some jewelry-quality beads and supplies.

The craft stores are good suppliers for basic beading materials, but if you want something special, go to the specialists. Check the Yellow Pages, local newspapers or bead magazines to find independent bead shops close to you or those that serve your area. They will probably be your best source for the widest variety from basic stock to unique beads and findings, to art glass and lampwork beads.

When visiting your local bead store, don't be afraid to talk to the owner. Many storeowners will happily tell you about the history of the beads you have chosen. It is a treasure to know about the lampwork artist who made the beads, or why the Venetians make their glass on the Islands of Murano, Italy, or what semiprecious stones were used to enhance the design.

Small independent shops are also a great source for inspiration. Many have samples to show and offer classes on various techniques. Specialty bead shops may also offer instant classes; a classroom or work area where customers may sit down and bead a project on the spot with help and support on-demand.

Other specialty shops that feature needlework, fibers and yarns may also be an unexpected source for beads. Art galleries and museum gift shops usually sell unique jewelry. Some sell art glass and lampwork beads by various artists.

If you are in search of that special bead, make sure to also look on the Web. The online retailers and the various Internet auction sites can be a valuable resource for inspiration and supplies. The Internet can help if you are not in an area with everything you need.

Bead magazines offer an astounding array of ads from people selling beads, either by catalog or online. Get copies of the latest beading magazines; you will find projects and advertisements from many suppliers who sell to the individual bead enthusiast.

Tips

● When you want the look of a metallic spacer without the expense, consider seed beads with metallic finishes or those that are lined in metallic foils.

● Search online auctions by typing into the search cue: "glass beads," "hanks of glass beads," "lampwork," "art beads," "seed beads" or "druks." When buying beads in online auctions, consider:

- The seller's feedback

- Shipping charges (seller's location)

- Handling charges (applied by seller)

- Purchasing more than one item from the same seller to save on shipping and handling costs

- A bead's actual size—photographs can be deceiving. When in doubt, ask. Reputable sellers will be happy to answer any of your questions.

- If the seller is offering items by the strand, ask for a bead count.

- Leaving positive feedback after a completed transaction.

● Bead magazines feature information on upcoming regional bead shows. The shows are organized like an open market, where you can see and purchase beads from a large number of vendors and artists. Check with the local chamber of commerce for details.

● Caveat Emptor

When shopping the Web for that special bead, beware. Sellers on eBay should offer full descriptions of beads, origin, quantity and size. If it seems too good to be true, it probably is. Be aware of the seller's shipping and handling charges. Sellers sometimes offer multiple items shipped together at no additional charge. While the charge may seem high for a single item, dividing the shipping may justify the cost.

Closer to Home

Don't forget to look for beads even closer to home, maybe the closest jewelry box. Some unique pieces are probably hiding in Mom or Grandma's jewelry box. With permission, of course, they may be just waiting for you to recycle them into a new creation. Be sure you are not cutting apart a priceless designer piece before beginning.

While you're at it, check your own jewelry box for outdated jewelry that you could take apart and use. You will probably find at least one or two necklaces or bracelets that you have not worn in years. They are just yearning to be reclaimed for a new creation.

Vintage pieces can be a great source for beautiful beads. The online auction sites also offer opportunities for you to buy vintage jewelry, sometimes at very good prices. If you don't already have vintage beads of your own, check out your local antiques shops and secondhand and resale stores. The stock is always changing and you never know what you may find. If you let the manager or owner of these shops know you are interested in glass beads, they will sometimes hold a new assortment for you to pick through before they send it to the floor.

Beads are also fun to trade. Having some friends over to bead may start a ruckus as you swap beads back and forth. It's half the fun of beading together. (The other half is sharing secrets and stories!) Don't be afraid to ask about sharing. We all have purchased beads and found that after making our next delectable piece of jewelry, we have plenty of beads left over.

Did you know?

● Ancient cultures believe that gemstones and beads have magical power. We are sure they can create laughter and friendship.

● Forget the chicken soup. If you have a friend who is ill, stop by with beads and bead board in hand. Our friends have told us many times that beading has helped heal. We believe.

A favorite recent piece with reclaimed beads (below right) started out life as a power bracelet (like the one at the left). These are great sources for some interesting stone beads and have enough matching beads to pull the color through a new design, whether you are creating a bracelet or necklace.

An antique brooch (like the one used in the necklace above, which is from the personal collection of Juli Ikonomopoulos) would be a real coup from a resale store and nothing sparkles like vintage crystal.

Cleaning Your Beads

Although there are likely many ways to effectively clean beads, the two options listed below are tried-and-true methods. For both, keep in mind that if you are reclaiming beads, you should cut them apart from the original strand before cleaning them.

Option 1

To clean loose beads, dental tablets work quite well. Drop your beads into a glass container with water and then drop in a tablet. A few minutes later you will have a lovely find. Test one bead before you immerse them. Sometimes beads have a reaction to the chemicals and will peel back. On those rare occasions, simply clean them in a mild soap and water solution.

Option 2

For glass beads, try a glass cleaner. Drop your separated beads into a plastic container. Add a mixture of three parts glass cleaner to two parts water and soak overnight. If the beads still need care the next morning, repeat the process with new glass cleaner and water. Once again, test this process on a few beads beforehand. Sometimes, you may mistake acrylics for glass. Acrylics do not like glass cleaner at all and may turn cloudy, so be careful. Test first.

Another Consideration

Always wash your hands before working with your beads. Crystals especially need TLC when it comes to cleaning them or working them into a design. The oils from your hands can collect on the beads and make them dull. Crystals need to be radiant, since that is their character, so treat them with special care. Commercial glass cleaner works exceptionally well for crystal beads.

When transporting crystals or storing crystal jewelry, separate them from other beads and beaded jewelry. The faceted edges of the crystals can be chipped or may scratch other beads and jewelry whether in transport or just sitting side-by-side in a jewelry box.

Vintage crystals are especially delicate. When buying vintage crystals, be sure to look at them under a loop (a jeweler's eyepiece). You will find fractures and missing corners on those whose care was less-than-perfect.

Storing Your Beads

When you have chosen and brought home your first beads, pull them out of the shopping bags and spread them out to admire. You will marvel at the array of beautiful colors, textures, sizes and how they capture the light. Then it hits you: How should you store these treasures?

From starting out with your first purchases in a plastic shoebox to finding the perfect containers for your ever-expanding collection, there are a lot of options out there to let you choose what's right for you.

First, be sure that your beads, supplies and tools are stored in a safe, dry place. They should be easily accessible to the area you will be using as a workspace. One word about workspaces—organize! Everyone would like to have a dedicated space to work on her hobby.

> ## Tip
> ● The nice thing about beading as a hobby is that the beads and tools are compact and easy to store, but organization is a must. If you are organized and store your materials close at hand, you will be able to spend more time enjoying your hobby, rather than searching for what you need.

Even if you only have a small space, you can have everything you need in one tackle box and store it in the bottom of a hutch, for example. Then it will be easy to pull it out and work on at the end of the dining room table next to a window for an hour or so before the kids come home from school or whenever you can.

Large plastic boxes with lids, like the shoebox type, may be right for you if your storage space is on a closet shelf. But remember: Beads can get heavy; don't store too large of a box on a high shelf. It's better to use several smaller ones. You can keep your stash in a small antique cupboard, for example, by using plastic divided boxes that fit and stack nicely according to the width of your shelves.

Be sure to keep beads away from small children. The colors and shapes may fool a child into thinking they are candy, so do keep them out of sight and on a shelf high enough not to be unexpectedly discovered by small children.

> ## Tips
> ● Thrift store and online auction beads can be great finds, but may require some work to unearth their beauty. If you are planning to restring them, cut away the old wire and place glass beads into a plastic container. Add a mixture of three parts glass cleaner to two parts water. Let them soak overnight. In the morning, the true beauty of the beads will shine through. (Always remember to test a few beads first.)
>
> ● A fascinating way to see your bead collection is to organize them into an antique-type tray. A lucky find at a flea market or antiques shop could make your collection a prominent display in your home.
>
> ● Gemstone jewelry should be stored in cloth bags. Gemstones are sensitive to heat and light and can easily be scratched by other jewelry.

Organizing Your Space

Choose a workspace and arrangement that is comfortable for you. You hear a lot about ergonomics these days and those concerns are well-founded when beading. Because beading can be consuming, you may be sitting longer than you realize. You will not do yourself any favors if you are hunched over your work for hours. So aside from getting up from your beading to move and stretch periodically, consider the following as well when organizing your workspace:

- A table or desk with a chair that is the correct height for you is essential.
- The work surface itself should be large enough to lay out your bead board, tools and bead box.
- Very good lighting is critical. A portable, true-color lamp, like the one illustrated below, is an excellent choice. It shows the colors and details of the beads, is great for color matching, and reduces eye fatigue.

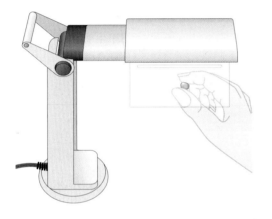

Clear, long storage tubes are ideal for keeping seed beads in various sizes readily accessible. The long, thin tubes often fit nicely in a larger storage box, like that shown here.

Choosing Containers

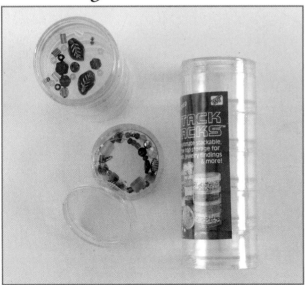

Clear, round containers are great for storing small amounts of beads. Some have snap tops, while others stack.

When shopping for containers, you'll notice most are clear or slightly transparent. That may be a little obvious, but when you can see inside the container, it becomes very user-friendly. Whether you choose containers that screw together, are round and stack, or are flat boxes with divided sections, the ability to see through them allows you to sort and choose colors and bead styles easily.

Clear containers are perfect for sorting by color groupings. Different specialty, novelty and accent beads can be stored together because they may be used together in the same project. For example, consider using a separate container for just blue and green beads. Put seed beads in separate boxes so you can pick out a different combination of colors to fill in any project.

Small zip-closure bags are a great way to sort beads or projects. They also layer nicely into a flat, clear box.

Remember that crystals should be stored separately. Try sorting lampwork beads by artist and art beads each in a separate container so you can quickly pick the focal inspiration for your next project.

Taking It With You

Many art stores carry a variety of suitable containers to allow for portability of your beading tools and supplies.

Tackle or portable toolbox types are very handy. They can hold small bead containers, as well as trays and stringing supplies.

Some rip-stop nylon totes, like those made by CIS (see Westrim in Resources, page 143), are designed to hold the plastic divided-container boxes.

Large plastic craft totes with handles are a good choice, too.

It's a good idea to keep tools and supplies in a small divided tote that also has room to carry along your latest project and an outside pocket to stash a bead board.

If you are traveling, there are several small convenient "carry-alls" that will keep your beads safe and sorted. Pharmacy pillboxes with small days of the week compartments are great for separating seed beads. Pill bottles keep small beads 3mm to 12mm safe. Of course, companies like FPC (Sure Bond) offer divided storage containers that are perfect if going on a vacation.

Always look for plastic storage containers where the dividers are permanently affixed and the lid closes flush to the top of the dividers. This way when the unit is raised for carrying, no beads will migrate and mix.

Portable plastic storage boxes with individual compartments make it easy to take your beading with you anywhere you go.

Tip

● Be sure to use secure containers to keep beads and supplies from being a temptation to small children or pets. If you have cats, its a good idea to cover your work area with a bath towel or blanket. If you are beading and get called away, then just cover your whole work area with the blanket to prevent any unwanted alterations to your progress.

Basic Toolbox

Once you have your fabulous beads in hand, there are only a few tools and basic materials required to complete a wonderful project.

Actually, there are only a few types of tools to consider when beading: cutters, pliers, and crimpers. With so few tools to get you on your way, make the most of your dollar. Look for tools that provide easy handling, such as those that are antiglare and have sure-grip, ergo handles.

Many of the tools are available through your craft or hardware stores in your local community. Check the garage first. Quite a few beading tools are used for repair around the house. The rosary or round nose pliers are called internal pliers at the electrical department in your local hardware store. Don't be afraid to investigate before you buy.

If you don't do repairs around the house, or your man won't part with any of his possessions, there are several craft and jewelry vendors who offer tool kits. Make sure to look at what you are actually buying. Some kits have added items not used in jewelry-making so the manufacturer can simply change the labels and sell the same kit for another craft. There is no sense in buying tools you will not use.

Jewelry and bead suppliers, including craft stores or catalog houses such as Rio Grande (see Resources, page 143), offer excellent choices. Buy the best tools you can afford. Remember: Tools should be comfortable to grip for long periods, so those with padded and/or textured handles are quite desirable.

The best cutters have tungsten carbide or titanium blades and are more durable than the alloyed variety. Look for cutters with flush blades used to get into tight spaces.

Look for tools with single or double springs. The springs add to a tool's durability and provide support for extended use.

Choosing the right set of tools can seem daunting. Here is a checklist that might assist you. Consider the following:

- Price
- Comfortable fit in your hand
- Small enough blades for extremely detailed work
- Strength of the blades
- Antiglare finish to prevent eye fatigue
- Spring tension for ease of use
- Resistance to rust in a humid climate

Bead happy!
Bring your inspiration, your beads and your tools.

Standard Tools

- Wire cutters
- Flat or chain nose pliers
- Needle nose or round nose pliers
- Journal for inspiration
- Bead board
- Honey pot
- True color light
- Various glues

Tips

● If you see nicks in your cutter blade, it generally means the blade is not strong enough for use with your wire. Only use cutters to their designated maximum cutting capacity.

● Tools are available especially for left-handed designers. See your supplier for specific details. (Rio Grande has a separate tool catalog with a lot of helpful information.)

What Tools to Buy

To begin, choose one wire cutter, one chain nose or flat nose pliers, and one round nose pliers (sometimes called needle nose or internal pliers). The basic tool kit is minimal, as the following list details. Of course you can get fancy and buy other tools and accessories. As far as a new hobby goes, the investment to begin beading can be very inexpensive and very portable.

Cutters

Cutters are used to cut flexible wire. They have very sharp blades.

Flat Nose or Chain Nose Pliers

Flat nose or chain nose pliers are reliable for crimping beads. Look for short jaws that are designed for delicate work. Tapered handles help in getting to tight spots. Never use serrated jaws.

Round Nose Pliers

Round nose pliers are used to create loops for earrings, dangles and spirals. Again, never use serrated jaws that can mar your finding's surface.

Journal

Carry a journal and colored pencils to retain ideas. Sometimes in setting out your beads, you will stumble onto more than one great pattern. It is a good idea to write down or draw your ideas for use on another project at a later time.

Carrying Cases, Trays and Containers

Choose one style and stick to it. Whether you prefer round, transparent containers or divided trays that come complete with cover for mobility, it is best to stay organized. Beads will seem to multiply at a fast pace and once you are into beading, having your supply organized and at hand at an inspirational moment's notice is imperative.

If you are planning to take your new hobby with you on a trip or over to a neighbor's for an evening of beading, try a portable toolbox. The hardware and craft stores carry several fine examples. Even when inspiration to make jewelry isn't with you, you'll enjoy sorting your stash. Sometimes you will rediscover a bead parked in a container from the past that is perfect for your next project.

The Honey Pot

A honey pot is a container where you can collect a number of styles, shapes, colors and sizes of beads for use in a project. Any container will do, but transparent white seems the best color. This avoids the risk of the color of the container influencing your assortment. Plastic ware is a good choice. A lid also helps with portability.

Muffin Tin

Once you have finished a project, return your beads to their rightful "homes." A muffin tin makes the sorting very simple and your task will be done quickly. Try sorting beads while on the phone with a friend or watching TV to take the "task" out of the job.

Various Glues

Some projects require glue. E6000 is a highly recommended glue. Also, be sure to have a quick-glue handy. Stick glue is great for gluing magazine and catalog ideas into your journal for inspiration at a later date.

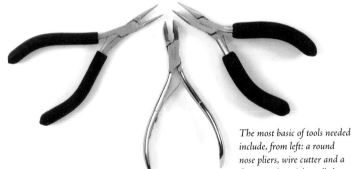

The most basic of tools needed include, from left: a round nose pliers, wire cutter and a flat nose pliers (also called a chain nose pliers).

Tips

● Never use scissors to cut flexible wire. Use a wire cutter and keep it safe in your toolbox, away from hubby and kids.

● Although actual crimping pliers are available, flattening a crimp with flat nose pliers has personally proven consistently more reliable.

Several varieties of honey pots.

Using a Bead Board

When you visit your favorite beadery, ask to see what bead boards they have available. Bead boards are available in a number of materials and widths. Some bead boards have separate areas to sort beads and findings. Many boards have more than one channel so that you can comfortably work on more than one strand of your project at once.

Most bead boards have rulers. The three- and four-channel trays provide a wide variety of uses, but always use the outermost channel when making a one-strand bracelet or necklace. The channels closer to the middle of the board are not as accurate. They work fine when reducing lengths for multi-strands, but can be deceptive when working on a single-strand piece.

Trays are available in a variety of finishes. Flocked trays are excellent for holding beads in place. If you get the urge to bead and your tray is not with you, use a terry cloth towel to lay beads out. The nap of the towel will hold the beads in place so your creativity can soar.

Which board is proper to use? Try several. Eventually you will decide which board is the most comfortable fit for each project. Many of the large craft chains offer these boards several times a year at reduced prices as incentives for bead artists to come visit their newest collections. Buy one or more. Remember to think about your work area. Make sure you can place the vertical board comfortably on your worktable. A board that is too large will have to be tilted to work with and that can be an unexpected annoyance, as well as a deterrent to your creativity.

Tip

• You can use a high nap terry cloth towel in place of a bead board if inspiration strikes when you are not at home.

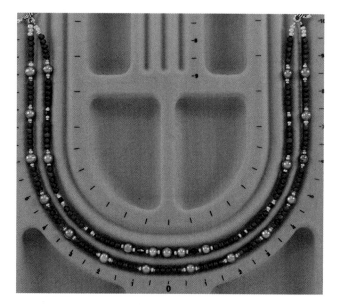

Let's Experiment

Once you have decided on a bead board that fits your needs, lay out a row of beads in the first channel. Use the "0" on the ruler (at the bottom of the board) as your center. Place beads on either side of the "0." You may choose to do either a symmetrical or an asymmetrical pattern. Lay beads in place as inspiration demands.

If you are planning to add seed beads to your creation, there will be no need to lay them out on the board first, unless your design requires much attention. Figure the number of seed beads required for your overall design (see seed bead chart, page 139) and leave enough room to accommodate their insertion.

Time to Try A Design of Your Own

Before beginning your project, try several arrangements of beads on your bead board. Once you have chosen a fabulous focal bead or set, make room for adventure. Using a honey pot, place your new acquisition in the center of the container and choose beads of varied size, shape, texture, sheen, transparency and color to fill in your creation. Varying size, shapes, textures and more can add more complexity to the work without the need to learn any fancy stringing techniques. Also, varying the color and transparency from the chosen focal bead can heighten or soften its appearance. Focal beads will take center stage if you use more monochromatic tones and smaller beads in a complementary color. Larger or brighter beads add movement and electricity to the pattern. Experiment. You will wear your piece of jewelry many, many times, so a little extra time spent choosing your pattern now can make quite a difference.

Keep a supply of jewelry ideas gathered from magazines and catalogs in your journal. Once you have collected many ideas for inspiration, you may wish to keep them clean and free from wrinkles, place them in acetate sheets and bind them in a three-ring, loose-leaf notebook. Whenever you need inspiration or a color suggestion, this loose-leaf and your journal with your own pencil sketches can serve as a guide.

Your first try may not be totally unencumbered. Realize this is your first piece and you are taking as friend, Noreen, calls them, "baby steps" to becoming the jewelry artist you wish to be. We promise you as soon as you see your results you will be back for more and this time with much less trepidation.

Things to Consider

When beginning your project, try several arrangements of beads. Once you have an assortment of 20 to 30 beads for your bracelet or 60 or more for a necklace, begin to lay your beads into a channel on the bead board. If you require a few more beads, you can easily return to your bead box. Don't forget to experiment. Half the fun of making jewelry is the experimental stage.

Some jewelry designers will actually string several repetitions of pattern in order to see how the design will look when strung. If you are having trouble visualizing the project from the bead board, try this method, as follows.

1. Cut 12" of flexible wire.

2. Place a knot at one end.

3. String one seed bead as a stopper, and then string several repetitions of your design.

Fabulous combinations of beads can be accomplished by assorting sizes, colors and shapes that are compatible into a container and then randomly laying handfuls of beads in whatever order they appear.

This technique is so rewarding, especially when it is a little late in the evening and you want to bead just to relax. There is little counting or sorting. It is fast and safe—and relaxing, since little thinking is involved. After you work with beads for a while, you come to love certain fill beads. There are certain 6/0 beads that I use over and over. You will come to know what pleases you by simple experimentation.

Stringing is basic.... You will feel the same excitement ...

Start by Stringing

Stringing is basic. Remember the days when you made necklaces from macaroni shells? The principal is the same. Today you will use better materials and learn to finish your piece by a different method than tying a knot, but all in all, not much has changed since those early days. You will feel the same excitement as you did when you first strung those macaroni shells.

Making a simple one-strand bracelet with a flexible wire and toggle clasp closure is a good way to begin beadwork. If you have worked with hemp, elastic or memory wire before, you will enjoy the more finished look that metal closures and flexible wire can bring.

The projects for this book are purposely simple and fun. The basic instructions outlined in the Single-Strand Basics section that follows may seem lengthy, but they include all of the tips and easy step-by-step information needed. There are no fancy techniques to learn.

Single-Strand Basics

Easy as 1-2-3

The three key steps to making your first piece of jewelry include:

1. Choose your design.

2. Crimp on one end of the closure and string your beads.

3. Slide on your crimp and the other end of your closure, check for proper fit and crimp your final crimp bead.

The average time to complete any simple bracelet will be approximately 30 minutes to one hour. Several suggestions follow for you to spend that time even more efficiently.

Use only precious metal crimps. They hold up better. Sterling silver crimps are more flexible and respond easily to flattening. Base metal crimps can sometimes crack and wear, leaving you to pick up handfuls of beads. Make sure the package says sterling. The word *silver* may only represent the base metal color. Also, if the crimps are too soft, the wire will eventually work its way loose. So, use a reputable brand of sterling silver crimps.

Use the best flexible wire you can find. Beadalon™ is strong and pliable. It comes in a number of colors, diameters and strengths. Try seven-strand .018-gauge silver-gray Beadalon for most of the projects in this book. If you encounter difficulty in finding any of the products recommended, check the Resources listing, page 143.

And, as with all things, enjoy what you are doing. If your budget requires you find beads that amount to less than $10, don't fret. This won't diminish the enjoyment of making your bracelet or the excitement of seeing your creativity soar. Just like with most crafts, it is the doing that really matters, and in the giving that is such a joy.

Did you know?

● Making jewelry is so easy. There are only three things you need to learn: how to start, how to string and how to finish. Are you unsure about starting? A simple bracelet takes about 20 beads and 20 minutes to make. Your first adventure can cost less than $10 and get you on your way to a new life as a jewelry designer.

30 Minutes to Emotional Bliss

"Beading is like therapy, only you get to leave with jewelry, too," says Brittany, a true bead enthusiast and friend. We can assure you it truly is 30 minutes to emotional bliss. There is something very special about beading. It is so simple; your mind can wander or get a quick respite from the day's activities, replete with the reward of a fabulous bauble. Something like a bubble bath with jewelry perks. We hope you will enjoy making beaded jewelry today.

Warning: This is addicting. Susan thinks she made 18 bracelets before she finally went on to something else. Just ask any of her friends. They all have one!

Making a Bracelet or Necklace

It is easy to start working with beads by making a bracelet. Most women have wrist sizes from 6½" to 8". If you are making a bracelet for yourself, simply use another bracelet from your jewelry case as your guide. If you are unsure of the size for a friend, use a 7" length of the beads as a starting point and adjust this to the overall size of the wearer. A petite woman might need a slightly smaller length and a large woman might require a longer length.

Also consider the size of the beads in your design. If your beads are extra large, their girth will take up extra room, as the bracelet will rest above the wrist instead of on it. So, when working with extra large beads, compensate for their size by adding some length. Of course, it is best to size the bracelet on the wearer before adding the finish clasp, but in most cases this is not possible.

Remember: If it doesn't fit, you can simply cut the wire (with wire cutters), carefully slide the beads one at a time back onto the bead board in proper order and restring the piece again. The second stringing will take little time, as the design will already be in place.

Another method of extending the size of a bracelet is to add an extender. An extender is usually made up of a small piece of chain or flexible wire between 2" and 6". The extender has an additional set of closures so it will easily attach to other finished jewelry.

The instructions for making a single-strand bracelet or single-strand necklace are the same. Only the length of wire and number of beads are different, so once you learn these basic steps, you are on your way.

Just a Few Basic Materials

Assorted beads: Gather 20 to 30 beads for a bracelet and 60 or more beads for a necklace, depending on their shape (with an average size of 6mm).

Bead board: Use one that will comfortably meet the needs of the size of your design, as well as your available work area.

Containers: Use a divided storage container, muffin tin or small jars for sorting beads.

Seven-strand .018 gauge silver-gray Beadalon flexible wire: How much wire? A good rule of thumb is 12" for a standard single-strand bracelet and 1 yard for the longest of necklaces or lariats or eyeglass holders. For a necklace and a bracelet set, plan on using at least 1 yard and up to 1⅓ yards. It is better to err on the side of more wire than less. When crimping an end that is short on wire, the task can get pretty labor-intensive. So, in this instance, more is better.

Split ring or jump ring: Use one in base metal: silver or gold. Split rings are more durable than jump rings.

Sterling silver, gold or vermeil crimp beads: Use two 2mm x 3mm in size and those made of precious metals, not base metal.

Sterling silver, gold or vermeil 3mm to 4mm seamless, round beads (optional): Use two beads to finish your bracelets and necklaces. Place them at each end of your project, just before the crimp bead to help the crimp bead withstand some of the pressure placed on it during wear.

Toggle or lobster clasp: Use a toggle set or lobster claw clasp with tab end in gold, silver, base metal, pewter or vermeil. (If the tab end is not available, use a jump ring or a split ring instead). Be careful when using base metal or pewter toggles; the metal is so soft it can sometimes be broken.

Designing Your Bracelet

● There are an infinite number of patterns you can use to make a simple bracelet.

Repeat pattern: A simple line of beads in a specific pattern running from one end of the bracelet to the other. There are many combinations you can create repeating bead after bead.

Centered: Start with the center bead and work each side from the center outward. We usually complete one side first and then simply match to the other side of the center bead.

Bead filler: We are very fond of using seed bead combinations to fill in between focal beads. They add color without weight.

Random: Pile a handful of beads onto your bead board and then into the channel in the order they appear, or place an assortment of beads in your honey pot and string in random order.

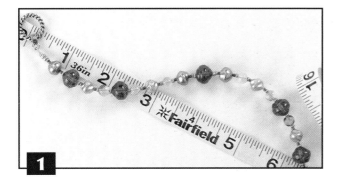

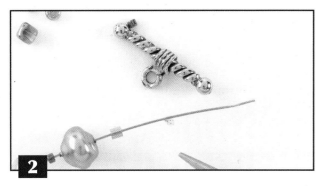

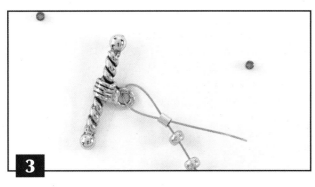

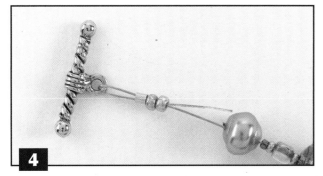

Single-Strand Bracelet Step-by-Step

1. Measure your wrist with a tape measure and then cut 12" of flexible wire from the spool. To determine the size of your finished bracelet, be sure to add length to compensate for your closure. your toggle with account for ½" to 1" of your finished work in most instances. If your wrist is more than 6½", add additional beads to your length. If your wrist size is smaller, use fewer beads.

2. To add the clasp to one end, string on the crimp bead to one end of the wire, allowing it to slide 2" from the end, and then string on one end of the clasp.

Tip

● If you are using a toggle, it is best to string the loop end first, as it will be easier when measuring your final fit. If you are using a lobster claw and tab, string the lobster claw first.

3. Holding the crimp bead in place, loop the end of flexible wire back through the crimp bead. Allow 2" of wire to pass through the crimp bead.

4. Take the end through the first two beads on the strand.

5. Pull the crimp bead up tight to the clasp.

6. With flat nose pliers, cover the crimp bead entirely and press down firmly to flatten the crimp bead.

7. Spin the crimp bead around and press down firmly again. Your crimp bead should be uniformly flattened on both sides. Test the closure by pulling firmly on the wire to be sure the crimp bead will hold.

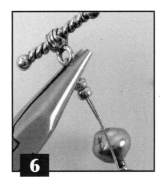

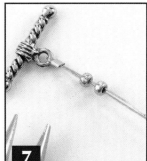

8. Slide the first beads up taut to your flattened crimp. Use wire cutters to clip the excess off the shorter wire end and discard the clipped piece.

● If you miscut your short "tail" wire, simply separate the last bead away from the others and clip the short wire again. Then, slide the bead back into place and continue stringing. Those little wires, if not completely hidden inside a bead, can be quite an irritant to your skin during wear, so it's best to be sure that they are hidden entirely.

9. String on beads, as desired. The first few beads on either end of your bracelet must have large enough holes to accommodate both strands of wire (so avoid ending with seed beads). But these beads must be small enough to easily fit through a toggle closure. Try using 6/0 or 8/0 beads for ending, if possible. As you go, check to be sure that your short wire has remained strung within the first few beads and that no beads are "hung up" on the wire.

● Sometimes beads resting on the bead board are not orientated properly and will actually take less room once strung. This especially happens with gemstone chips, which are odd shapes. At rest, the chips will appear to occupy more space than they actually do. So measure twice and crimp once.

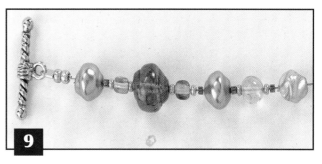

10. Finish the strand as you began, stringing on small beads, followed by the crimp bead and clasp. Loop the end of the wire back through the crimp and two round beads.

● If this is your first bracelet, before completing step 10, try it on. Hold the open end firmly, or ask someone else to hold it for you, and wrap the bracelet around your wrist to see if your measurements were accurate.

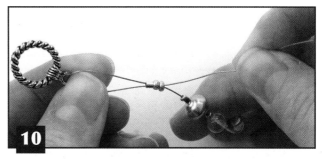

11. Once the wire has cleared the first several beads, you can begin to pull the wire taut. Be sure to string through clasp, crimp and metal beads or other beads all at once. When the wire is taut it becomes difficult to string through additional beads.

● It is easiest to pull the wire through the crimp, silver bead and end beads in step 11, if you can keep the crimp bead away from the clasp end as you go. Slide the crimp bead as close to the beads as you can while you feed the wire through. Sometimes, if enough wire remains, you can simply feed the loop until most the wire has been strung in place. Other times you will need the aid of the flat nose pliers to hold the short end of the wire and pull it taut as you go.

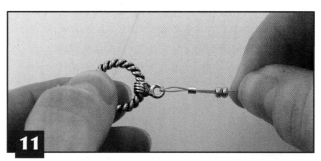

12. Snug the crimp and end beads close to the toggle, pulling on the end of wire to tighten any gaps in the design.

Tip

● If you are stringing heavy glass or natural beads, you can insert crimp beads every 3" or 4". Crimp as you go. Such crimps add much-needed security so your piece will stay crimped. Crimps can be hidden inside beads or spacers, so as not to be visible to view.

13. Once the short wire has been pulled as far as possible, hold the bracelet vertically with the finished end down, make sure no space remains between any of the beads. Sometimes a bead will get "hung up" on the wire and more often than not, won't be discovered until after you have crimped your second crimp bead unless you take the time now to inspect your work. Check again for proper fit on your wrist before crimping. Remember: Measure twice and crimp once.

14. Pull on the wire one last time to remove any slack. Flatten the final crimp, as the first one in steps 6 and 7.

15. Trimming the final wire takes care, as the beads are now nestled together. Separate the beads where the small wire "tail" rests into a 45-degree angle. Cut away the "tail" wire by holding the flush side of the wire cutter as close to the wire cutter as you can. Make sure the beaded wire remains away from the cutter to avoid cutting into the bracelet.

   • Sometimes the shortened "tail" wires split out of the beads near an end of your design after some wear. Place a tiny string of super glue on the wire and re-insert into the beads. Allow the glue to set up. Your wire will now stay in place.

Once you have completed a bracelet that fits you properly and know exactly where you would like it to rest on your wrist, you can use this bracelet for a pattern for other bracelets you would like to make. This is still a "trial-and-error" technique. Everyone has an imaginary point on his or her wrist that feels right, so it is best to have the wearer try on a few bracelets before making one for a friend.

Once your bracelet is complete, you might put it on a flat bed scanner and scan the bracelet full size. It is fun to note the exact size of the bracelet, the date it was made, the person who owns it, the types and the origins of the beads, their makers and where the beads were purchased. You can even keep a scrapbook of all of the beaded work you do. It will be a fond memory of how much you will learn over the years, as well as document where many beads originated or who now proudly wears your designs.

Other Ways to Secure Your Wire While Stringing

In the previous directions, one end of the toggle is attached to the wire at the beginning before you start stringing your beads. This end acts as a stop while you are stringing.

As an alternative, you can use a hemostat (medical clamp) to secure one end of the wire while you string. Using a hemostat lets you try on the strung bracelet before adding crimps and toggles. If the bracelet is too long, you can remove the hemostat and easily remove a few beads. If it is too short, you can add a few beads—all without having to remove the one toggle end closure. The serrated edge of the hemostat will bend the wire, so always place the clamp at the farthest possible end of the wire so it can be trimmed later.

Another way to temporarily secure the end is to simply slide a seed bead onto the wire, then tie a knot so the seed bead rests in the center of the knot to act as your stop.

One real advantage to the technique of using a clamp or a knot instead of an attached toggle comes when you are working a centered design. If you need to lengthen or shorten your pattern to fit, you will need to adjust the same beads on each side to match. The clamp will help you do this much more quickly than sliding your beads completely off the wire. We find it to be a favorite, too!

Tip

• Hemostats serve a wealth of tasks. This handy clamp is a good tool to have. Any flea market will have at least one dealer with boxes of them, so pick some up out there today. You won't regret it. If you can't find a flea market, try eBay.

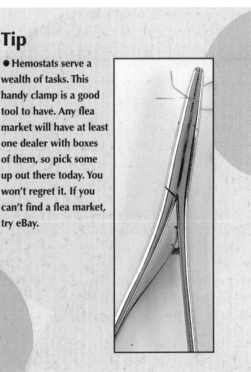

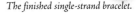

The finished single-strand bracelet.

Single-Strand Necklace Tips

To make a single-strand necklace, the steps are the same as a single-strand bracelet with the only difference being the length of the finished piece. Use the steps below to determine length for your necklace.

1. To determine the size of your finished necklace, choose the length you want from choker to longer necklace (see Jewelry Lengths chart, page 141).

2. If you are making a choker, measure your neck with a string at the position you want the necklace to rest.

3. Add 1" to your neck measurement for the correct size of your finished necklace length.

4. Take the desired finished necklace length and add 4" to determine the length of wire to cut.

Tip
● If your beads are exceptionally large, you may need to add more length to compensate for the additional diameter of the large beads. Plan for more wire accordingly.

Growing Your Design

Extending a beaded bracelet to create a necklace design is very simple.

1. Lay your bracelet in the second channel of your bead tray.

2. Find and assort beads that are the same as or similar to the bracelet beads.

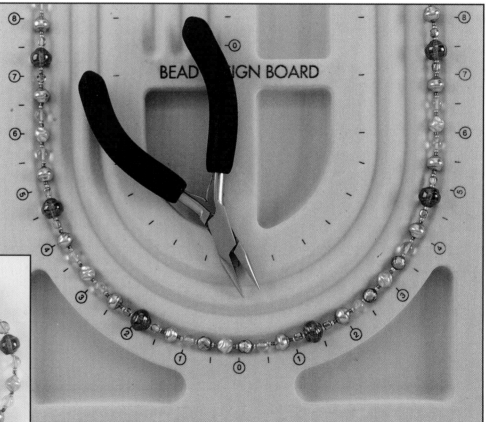

Whether continuing the pattern of the bracelet for your necklace or making a whole new look, laying the work onto the first channel of the bead board allows you to play with the different options before spending the time stringing.

3. Duplicate the bracelet design by repeating the chosen beads, placing them into the first channel of the bead tray.

4. Make some decisions about the design. Is the necklace long enough? Do you want to continue the same pattern up the rest of the necklace?

5. If you decide to continue the same pattern up the rest of the necklace, which happens to be the easiest method. Move your bracelet to the left or right of the existing new necklace pattern and continue to copy the pattern until you have reached the desired length.

6. Do you want to alter the pattern as it continues up the necklace? Start with the same beads that you used to duplicate the bracelet. Alter them on either side of the newly created portion of the necklace. You will be able to play with the arrangement until you are comfortable with the way the necklace is evolving.

Remember to take into consideration whether the necklace will be under a shirt collar and could become uncomfortable if the beads are too large higher up the neckline and under the collar. This is the reason that some necklaces graduate the size of the beads to smaller and smaller beads as they reach the back of the neck. You may decide to keep the original pattern at the front of the necklace only and use much smaller beads to continue up the neckline. If you create a consistent smaller pattern away from the original, you will add emphasis to the original design.

Other opportunities abound. Try experimenting again. You will find an endless offering of ideas for extending the necklace to its new length.

Maybe you would like to add some other beads that were not used in the original bracelet. Simply move aside some of the duplicated design and insert some of the new additions to a portion of the new necklace. Then continue to add the new beads every so often up the neckline.

When making a necklace, consider how it will lay on your neck and upper body. Collarbones offer an opportunity to show off the delicate nature of the beads below and above it by how the beads lay in place.

Consider, too, if the wearer will be wearing an open back, as with a bridal or other formal piece or even some summer casual. If so, you may want to add additional interest in the back of the necklace with a chain or a dangle. A special-occasion dress such as a strapless gown may be the opportunity for a necklace that has dangles or drops all the way around.

Tips

● When making a pendant from an object without a hole, use silver wire to secure it. Make a loop twice as large as you will require. Wrap the wire several times around the object, continuing to make a loop twice the size. Once you have done this three or four times, leave about 1" of extra wire and cut the rest away. Holding the loop, twist the wire around and around, creating a wire figure eight. When the wire is taut, wrap the short end around the twist—and voila!—a pendant.

● You can now find bead sets in graduated sizes for use in your project. Mail-order catalogs may be your most likely resource.

Multi-Strand Basics

In designing a multi-strand project, keep in mind that to get the same fit as you have with a single strand bracelet or necklace, you will need to allow for a little additional length in wire and also a few additional beads.

Same length: The strands may be the same length, but they will need to be slightly longer than a single strand by itself, because the multi-strands take more room to sit together on top of the wrist or neck, and also more slack is taken up by all the strands coming together at the clasp.

Torsade: The strands are all of equal length and before you hook the clasp to wear it, you twist the strand several times. This can be a very elegant look, but it does take quite a bit more length to allow for the twist.

Graduated: Each strand can be graduated in length so that when worn, the strands are next to each other in order. This is a flattering look in any length necklace.

The twisted or graduated strand technique is very easy to achieve with a multi-channel bead board. The outside channel, or the one closest to the edge of the board, is the longest and the most accurate for length.

You will find fun challenges in designing a necklace with more than one strand. Try repeating a design element from the center of the shorter strand onto the sides of a longer strand for a start to a formal symmetrical design. Repeating a design element or even a particular bead will help pull a design together. Multiple strands that are all different can be fun and may have a more casual feel. Experiment and have fun.

Multi-strands, like the necklace design by Brittany Berndtson shown above, use the same technique as a single-strand except that you add more strands to your closure or split ring.

Making a Multi-Strand Bracelet

To complete a multi-strand bracelet with equal length strands, repeat the instructions specified in Single-Strand Basics, pages 23-29, for each strand of the bracelet, completing one strand at a time. The only difference is in adding 1" to your measured wrist length in step 1. Also, when you lay out your patterns of beads on the multi-channel bead board, alternate large and small beads on strands that will be next to each other, as the prominence of focal beads will be enhanced and larger beads will not collide with each other.

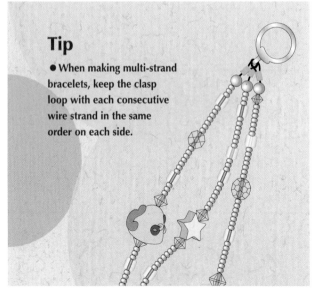

Tip

● When making multi-strand bracelets, keep the clasp loop with each consecutive wire strand in the same order on each side.

Use the how-to photos here for additional guidance, if necessary, as you finish the second strand.

1. Attach the second strand with small beads and the crimp bead.

2. Loop wire through the clasp and back through the crimp and first three beads on the strand, just as with the first strand.

3. Finish just as before by pulling the crimp snug to the clasp, checking the length around your wrist, flattening the crimp bead on both sides and snipping the excess wire tail.

Tip

● Try using seed beads to fill in one or two strands. On a five-strand bracelet, using seed beads for the second and fourth strands can make the focal beads more prominent. Another choice for filler beads might be heishe 3mm or 4mm beads. The choice of heishe beads has become very popular in some fashion catalogs of late.

● If you have enough excess wire length, you can wait to flatten the final crimp on each strand until you are finished with all the strands. This gives you one last chance to alter the lengths. Take care to not pull on already finished strands while checking their length. When you are finished stringing, check that each wire is taut, and flatten the crimps.

● It's worth repeating: Be sure your strands are in the same order on the clasp on each end of your necklace.

● Remember to vary color, texture, transparency, size and shape of your beads when building your necklace.

Multi-Strand Necklace Tips

To complete a multi-strand necklace or choker, follow the multi-strand bracelet instructions, page 30. The only difference is in first determining what style necklace you'd like (same length, graduated strands or torsade) and then cutting each wire strand accordingly. A multi-channel bead board will help you determine the number of beads in each strand. It is always good to be generous with your wire and then trim later so you won't be disappointed. Once you have decided on the finished length for your desired necklace, add 4" to determine the wire length to bead each strand.

From base metals to precious metals ... and everything in between.

Findings
and Closures

There is no closure easier than no clasp at all. A lariat design loops through itself or the two ends can be gently tied together in an overhand knot allowing the ends or tassels to hang free.

Other types of findings and closures are almost infinite, from base metals to precious metals and reclaimed antique clasps to contemporary toggles and everything in between. You will find something perfect for every project.

Toggles

Toggles seem to be a favorite style to use for bracelets. A toggle is very easy to fasten with just one hand when trying to put on jewelry by yourself.

Toggle clasps can be tricky when attaching multiple strands. Be sure that the bar-end of the toggle can fit comfortably through the ring with the beads on the strand. Beads that are too large near the bar-end may prevent it from threading through the ring. To be sure, cut your wire additional lengths, then string your beads, thread on the crimps, but do not crimp. The extra length will secure the beads while you try on the piece. Once you are happy, thread the short end of wire through beads and crimp. Flatten the crimp and trim the wire.

When choosing a necklace clasp, be sure it is secure for the weight or number of strands. Also consider how it will feel on the back of the neck. The projects for this book are purposely simple and fun. The basic instructions outlined in the Single-Strand Basics section, pages 24-29, may seem lengthy, but they include all of the tips and easy step-by-step information needed. There are no fancy techniques to learn.

Toggle clasps come in a wide variety of styles. Think about how the clasp you choose can work with and enhance your overall bracelet or necklace design.

An example of a lariat-style necklace, the Lilacs in Bloom project, shown here and detailed on page 131, shows the simplicity such a design has to offer, as it does not require a closure.

Button-and-Loop Closures

One interesting, inexpensive closure can be made from a shank button and a beaded loop. Here's how to start stringing your piece with a button loop closure:

1. Cut the desired length of wire and thread a crimp bead onto it.

2. Thread on an odd number of seed beads. The length that the seed beads cover the wire should equal ¼" more in length than the diameter of the button you are wiring. This will allow the button to slide through the loop.

3. After you have threaded the appropriate number of seed beads, thread your wire back through the crimp.

4. Pull on both wires together, as you push the crimp toward the loop of seed beads to remove any slack.

5. Flatten the crimp.

6. String your strand as usual, covering your tail of wire next to the crimp with two or three beads.

7. On the other end, attach the button just as you would any other clasp.

The finished loop.   The finished button end.

Bracelet and Necklace Extenders

If you would like to attach a piece of chain for an extender to the end of your bracelet or necklace, you may want to create it with split rings or jump rings and an additional lobster claw clasp.

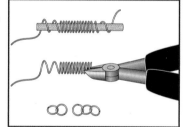

Tip

● If you are stringing heavy glass or natural beads, you can insert crimp beads every 3" or 4". Crimp as you go. Such crimps add much-needed security so your piece will stay crimped. Crimps can be hidden inside beads or spacers, so as not to be visible to view.

Jump Ring Closures

Check to see that the gauge of the jump ring is heavy enough to secure attachments.

When opening a jump ring, take care not to lose the tension of the circle. The best way to open a jump ring is to use two pairs of pliers, one in each hand, as follows:

1. With the circle facing you, gently grasp each side of the jump ring next to the opening.

2. Push one side of the jump ring away from you while pulling the other one toward you. This side-to-side motion keeps the integrity of the circular shape. Pulling the ends away from each other would distort the ring.

3. While open, slide the ring through your attachments or connections.

4. Push the ends of the jump ring back to center to close.

When using a jump ring, be sure to check that it is completely closed. Even the smallest opening can come apart and could allow any attachments to come loose. When using precious metals, jewelers will solder jump rings closed.

Tip

● Broken clasp? You may not need to restring it. Simply place a split ring or jump ring through the loop at the end of the flexible wire next to the crimp. Then you can safely cut away the broken clasp. Secure the new clasp to the split ring.

Other Closures

Closures can be used in unconventional ways. The following are some more specialized examples of closures and how they can be used.

Eyeglass Holders

Here are some examples of chains for your eyeglasses. They are great for "cheaters" or even sunglasses. The closure that attaches to hold the glasses secure is similar to a rubber gasket and can be rolled on or off the end of the eyeglass bow.

To keep the chain secure and out of the way while wearing it, many people slide the chain up onto the temple part of the bow. Check for yourself where you would like the beads to fall. If the chain is for a pair of cheaters you wear all the time for reading, you may want smaller beads in the first 3" close to the bow so as not to obstruct your view. Chunkier, bright beads all over are a very fun look to accessorize your sunglasses. You might want to graduate to smaller size beads around the back of the neck for comfort.

The closure on these eyeglass chains is attached the same way you would attach a clasp at the end of a necklace.

1. When you are finished stringing your design, string on a crimp bead, thread the wire through the closure and back through the crimp bead and a couple of beads.

2. Pull taut.

3. Flatten the crimp.

4. Trim the wire.

5. Repeat on the other end. Sometimes these loops are strung with seed beads so not to expose the wire.

You can find eyeglass holders in several departments of your local craft store. First try the bead department. Usually eyeglass holders are sold with other bead findings, but sometimes they are available in the sewing supplies department of fabric centers.

Lorgnette and ID Holder

A lorgnette is a necklace to keep your magnifying glass handy. Since the strand is so long and can be looped over the head, no regular closure is necessary and crimp beads are used in front to secure the beaded strand to the magnifying glass pendant.

Try a casual necklace to serve as a strap for an ID badge holder. Once again, the clasp is in front to secure the holder. As with all the funky projects shown on this page, when laying out your design, remember that the center of the strand you are beading will actually fall at the back of the neck so plan on your smallest beads there.

Tip

● The closure on this particular lorgnette and badge holder is similar to the button loop closure. Because the hole isn't large enough to accommodate both wire and seed bead, when you are threading on your seed beads, only thread on half, then thread your wire through the clasp (or in this case the end of the magnifying glass) then thread on the rest of the seed beads and back through your crimp. Finish as a button loop

● If you are making an ID holder for an existing badge, you can cut away the cording from the existing badge. Bead on a new piece of flexible wire.

Notice how similar the two loops at the ends of the strand for the lorgnette are a button-and-loop closure.

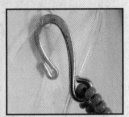

Attach an S-hook to the looped end of the badge holder strand and see how easily it attaches to the nametag.

Eyeglass holder designs by Linda Zsevc.

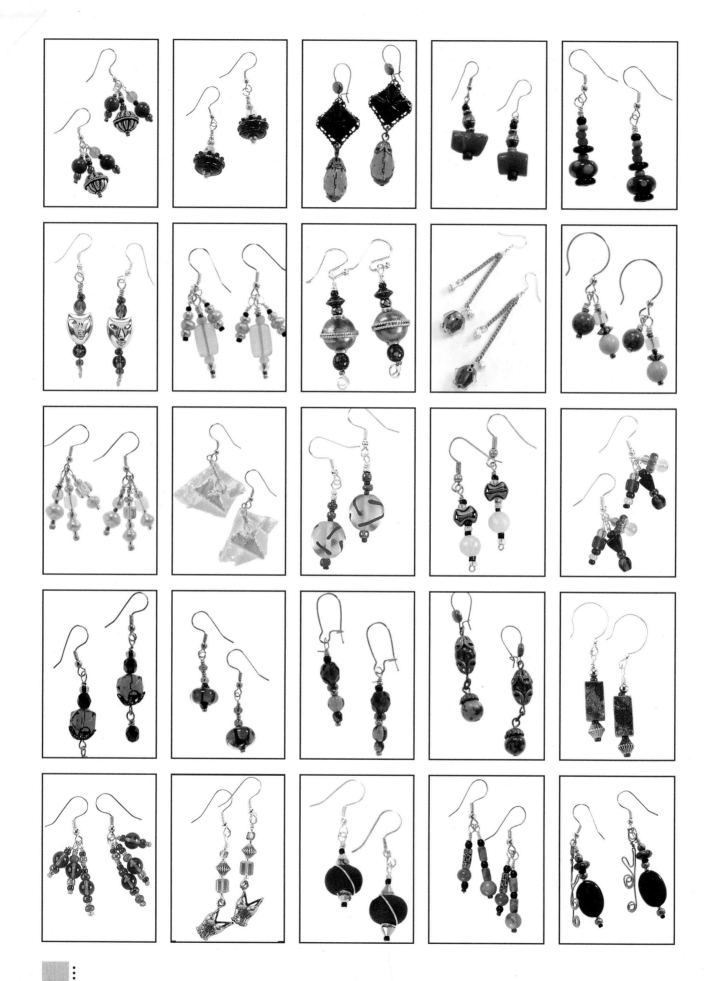

Earring and Dangle Basics

Learning to make earrings is easy and the quickest jewelry project. Earrings are a great pick-me-up to coordinate your outfit or a fast gift for a friend.

Earrings are also a great way to showcase special beads. You can buy just two matching lampwork or vintage beads and let them draw attention to your winning smile.

The basic component you need to be able to make earrings is a dangle. The technique you need to learn to make dangles is how to "twist" the wire at the top, which is sometimes called a rosary turn or wrapped loop. This is a wonderful skill to learn because you can use it for so many things. Whether you just want to make a simple pair of earrings, add a tassel to the clasp of your necklace or bracelet, or dangle a hundred beads on a cha-cha bracelet, this method will get you there. It does take practice and some patience. Don't give up.

Use only sterling silver or other precious metal headpins when making earrings. You will be frustrated if you try to use base metal pins. Even experienced designers find that base metal does not make for a good turn.

Practice makes perfect. The best suggestion is that you take the time to practice this technique. Most people must turn at least 50 dangles before they can say that they have mastered the rosary turn. Using finer wire is essential to getting the proper look of the turn. We recommend the wire hardness of half-hard 22-gauge sterling silver wire.

Making a Rosary Turn (Wrapped Loop) on a Dangle Step-by-Step

Let's begin with a dangle that is prepared first and then added to your earrings or necklace later. You will need sterling or vermeil headpins in 2" to 4" lengths.

Although some can comfortably make this turn with 2" headpins, you may prefer 3" to 4" lengths. You will be trimming off the excess, so you can use shorter headpins if you like; however, it is easier to maneuver good turns on a rosary turn when you have a longer tail to work with.

It is a lot easier to work "off-line" when learning this technique. Once you have the technique down, you can actually do them directly onto the earring wires or necklace.

Toolbox

- Round nose or needle nose pliers
- Sharp wire cutters (for cutting sterling silver wire)
- Flat nose pliers

Tip

● The smaller, more delicate the cone on the round nose pliers, the more delicate the results will be on the turn.

Tips

● If French ear wires don't stay in your pierced ears, tiny plastic discs that go behind your ears will help.

● You can create your own ear wires by making a simple jig of a favorite design and wrapping half-hard sterling silver wire around it. As you become more experienced, you will know if you require hard or soft sterling wire instead. The favorite coil and ball can be added to get a really professional look. Coils and small 3mm to 5mm silver balls are sold separately by Rio Grande and Fire Mountain Gems (see Resources, page 143), or may be found in your local bead shop. You can also use niobium wire on a jig to make your own ear wires. Niobium is a hypoallergenic metal that came from the space industry. More importantly, it comes in many cool colors.

● Earrings make great fundraisers! Teach a few friends to make a rosary turn. Put on a good movie and before you know it, you will have made 100 or more pairs. If one friend can't accomplish the rosary turn, let her open and close the earring loops.

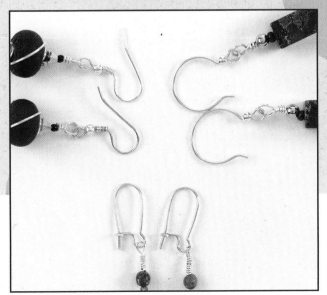

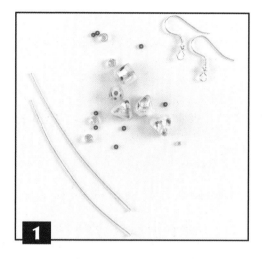

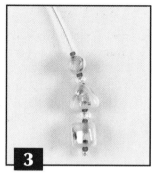

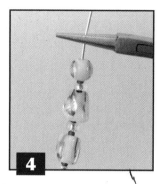

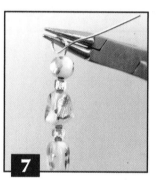

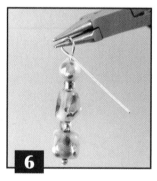

1. Assemble the items needed for your earrings: two headpins, two ear wires and enough beads to make matching patterns on both of the dangles.

2. String the beads onto the headpin using the tiny head of the pin as the base of the dangle. If your first bead is too large and falls off the head of the pin, try stringing a small transparent 10/0 or 11/0 seed bead or a 2mm to 3mm silver or gold bead on the end first. This will help hold the larger bead in place.

3. Stop adding beads when you have approximately 1" (or more) of the pin showing.

4. Place your round nose pliers approximately ¼" from the top of the last bead. Grasp the pin tightly with the pliers.

5. Using your thumb and forefinger, bend the wire over the back of your pliers

6. Cross the wire underneath and in front of the stationary wire, forming the start of the loop.

7. Bring the wire forward, beginning the first complete turn.

8. Grasp the newly formed loop with the pliers and turn the loop several times to provide three neatly spaced turns. Some people choose to turn the wire instead of the loop, but we have had the best results by turning the loop itself. This seems to give a more precise finish to the work.

9. When the turns are completed, cut away the remainder of the wire.

10. Grasping the loop, tuck the newly cut end down and in toward the top bead with your flat nose pliers.

11. Now your dangle is complete and can be strung onto the wire.

Adding on the Ear Wires

When making earrings, complete your dangles first. Be sure they match by holding them side-by-side. Place them on an ear wire that opens by following these steps:

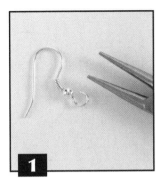

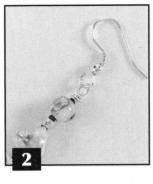

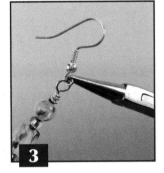

1. With round nose pliers, gently open the loop on the ear wire by twisting it slightly to the side. Try opening at the front or back of the loop. Do not pull it apart, as it will be very difficult to close.

2. Slide on your dangle.

3. Close the loop with the round nose pliers.

4. To regain symmetry, press the loop gently between blades of a flat nose pliers for the finished look, as shown.

Once you have accomplished the rosary turn, you should practice doing the turn directly onto the loop of a pair of French ear wires. To do so, "thread" the French ear wire loop onto the headpin before you bend the loop down and forward. Once the earring loop is in place, keep it out of the way while you complete the turns.

There are many other earring findings that can be substituted for French ear wires; however, French ear wires remain the most popular. The technique does not change. Follow the same instructions for drop, post or lever-back earrings, either making the dangle first or making it directly onto the ear wire as necessary.

A Word About Eyepins

Eyepins serve to add "joints" to your dangles and extend an earring dangle's length. Here's how:

1. String your beads on your headpin as directed in the previous rosary turn step-by-step instructions.

2. With round nose pliers, open the eyepin premade loop just enough to slip on the newly formed loop of the headpin.

3. Close the premade loop securely and continue to string more beads on the eye pin.

4. Leave at least 1" of pin to make a second rosary turn.

5. Create a second rosary turn as before and attach to an ear wire, as shown in the photo at left.

6. Attach your dangle to bracelets or necklaces using a jump ring.

Tip

● When you make earrings or dangles, use a guide on your left index finger and on the tips of the round nose pliers. Using a permanent fine point, black marker, create a ¼" line on the inside of your finger. Choose a spot on your pliers and mark it. (The permanent marker will likely not remain on the pliers, but can serve as a temporary guide.) This helps to keep the size of the loop and the wrap consistent.

Other Uses for Dangles

Dangles can be used to embellish pieces other than earrings. The projects in this book include some examples from a single pendant with dangles to a charm bracelet to a cha-cha bracelet.

The cha-cha bracelet is one of our favorites; you can make the dangle directly on the loops of the cha-cha bracelet base or you can make them separately and attach them with jump rings. Either way, it will give you lots of practice with dangles and a very fun way to display your work.

Tip

● When attaching dangles to the end of a bracelet near a toggle clasp, always attach the dangle to the ring-end (not the bar-end) of the toggle. You will not be able to thread the bar through the ring if the dangle gets in the way. Putting the dangle on the ring-end prevents this problem from happening.

● Indulge yourself. Add beads to your old charm bracelet. The textural richness of so many beads will highlight the gold and silver charms.

● Cha-cha bracelets can become a collector's item. If you use the bracelet to highlight each bead in your collection, it can become a helpful (as well as colorful) reminder of a bead you need to match.

● If you have a color grouping you have enjoyed, make up a 4" headpin of the beads, leaving 4" of pin to turn a loop. Then save your samples on a key ring or tassel bookmark.

Pendants can be attached by using the same method as creating an earring dangle and if you like, you can embellish the pendant even further with fringe-like dangles at the bottom, like those here.

Try using many dangles of the same beads to create a striking necklace, like the Flaneur Choker shown here and detailed on page 84.

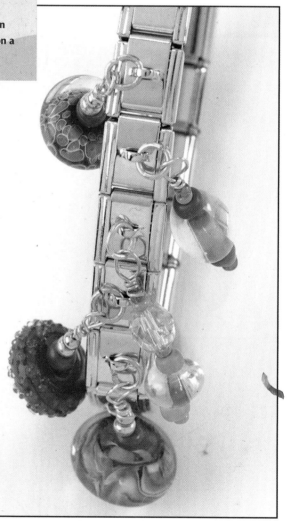

Making a cha-cha bracelet provides a fun way to practice dangle-making for a unique end result.

Memory Wire

Memory wire is a fun, quick way to bead with a different look. Instead of using flexible wire, the wire used comes in a coil like a spring or a "slinky."

It is called memory wire because even after stringing beads onto it, the wire doesn't lose its coil shape. Memory wire comes in sizes to make necklaces, bracelets and rings. It may come pre-cut in a package or as a coil long enough for several projects.

When measuring for how much wire to use for bracelets, figure about one-and-a-half loops of wire will expand to about one wrap by the time the beads are threaded on it (depending on the size of the beads).

So, for example, for a bracelet that wraps around your wrist twice, count out a three-loop coil. Speaking of cutting, this wire is very tough. You will need a heavy-duty (hardware) cutter for memory wire. Do not ruin your good jewelry cutters trying to conquer this task.

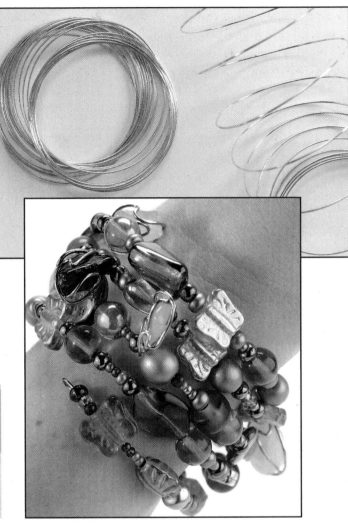

Tip

● Use a sturdy pair of pliers. Protect your hands from the sharp ends of the memory wire by wearing gloves. If you can't seem to turn the wire on your own, ask a kind gent for assistance. Use E6000 glue to secure a memory wire bead tip (cap).

1

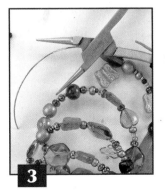
2

3

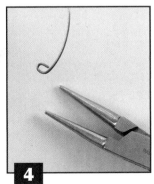
4

Memory Wire Step-by-Step

1. Cut a coil with the number of loops desired.

2. Use pliers to bend one end of the wire into a loop, as shown. This will act as a stop.

3. Thread beads onto the memory wire coil sliding them down to the loop.

4. Make a loop on the other end to secure.

One nice touch is to add dangles hanging off the loops on either end. Another finishing technique, instead of loops on either end, is to glue (E-6000) a bead to each end. You can use half-drilled beads or end caps especially made for memory wire (see Resources, page 143).

Tip

● Memory wire is great for making beaded wraps with lots of uses. We've used the bracelet size to decorate candles, candleholders and vases, and the ring size to make napkin holders and matching wine glass charms. The sky's the limit!

Moss Pearls and Chips Double-Strand Bracelet

Designer: *Sue Wilke*

Finished Size: 7" without clasp
Where to Get It: Specialty bead shops or catalogs; on the Web
Time to Complete: One afternoon
How Much Will It Cost? A movie and popcorn (under $20)

What You Need
82 moss green matte 8/0 seed beads
5 green freshwater
  6mm x 9mm potato-shaped pearls*
4 green freshwater 7mm x 4mm
  rice-shaped pearls*
3 gold/yellow freshwater 6mm x
  5mm rice-shaped pearls*
17 tiger-eye chips*
25 rhodonite chips
4 gold 2mm x 3mm crimp beads
Gold toggle set
2 11" lengths flexible wire
*Available through Fire Mountain Gems

Toolbox
Wire cutters
Flat nose or chain nose pliers

What You Need to Know
See the instructions and information outlined in Single-Strand Basics, pages 23-29, and Multi-Strand Basics, pages 30-31.

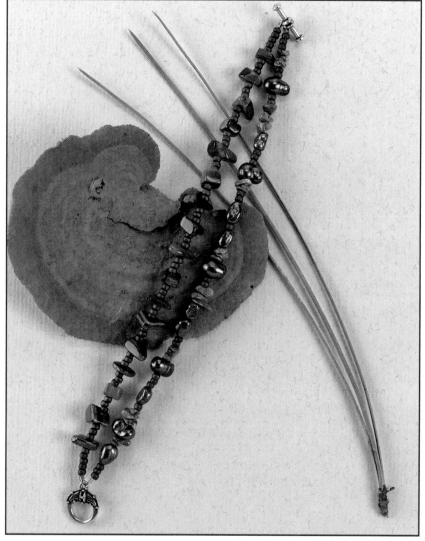

Glowing tiger-eye chips enhance the olive, copper and brown cultured freshwater pearls and matte olive seed beads in this delicate two-strand bracelet.

Tip
●Natural stones, fresh water pearls and crystals can be porous. Be sure to put them on after you use hair spray, perfume or nail polish remover, as each can damage bead finishes.

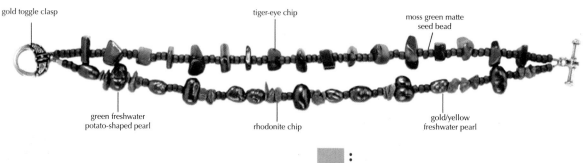

gold toggle clasp

tiger-eye chip

moss green matte
seed bead

green freshwater
potato-shaped pearl

rhodonite chip

gold/yellow
freshwater pearl

Mountain Pacific Necklace

This necklace reads like a good cook's stew along the trail. Be sure to blend all these heartwarming ingredients: hand-cut malachite, sterling silver, nickel spacers, vintage Venetian glass and crystals, pava beads, designer lampwork and a buffalo nickel button clasp for good measure.

Designer: *Susan Ray*
Lampwork Artist:
Tamara Knight

Finished Size:
21½" without clasp
Where to Get It: Specialty
bead shops or catalogs;
on the Web
Time to Complete:
One afternoon
How Much Will It Cost?
A manicure ($20 to $50)

What You Need to Know

See the instructions and information outlined in the Single-Strand Basics, pages 23-39, and the Button-and-Loop Closures section, page 34. When making a button-and-loop closure, you need to compensate for the additional length of the loop end in relation to the button, so that your design will remain centered. In this project, the loop end is strung with only one 3mm round next to the crimp, while the button end has three 3mm rounds to compensate.

Did you know?

● Venetians had the good fortune to discover, by chance, the use of copper crystals in glass decoration (known as owen turine or goldstone), assuring their position as skilled bead makers. Today, the technique is produced around the world.

What You Need

12mm x 18mm lampwork rondelle disc	4 pewter 7mm x 7mm spacers
85 silver-lined smoke 8/0 seed beads	2 vintage white 9mm potato-shaped pearls
6 green transparent 6/0 seed beads	2 moss green 18mm x 10mm lampwork rounds
35 copper shiny 13/0 seed beads	2 clear/amethyst 8mm rounds
6 hand-cut malachite 8mm to 9mm rounds	2 brass 4mm x 10mm rondelles
8 wood 10mm x 8mm barrels	2 Bali silver 4mm x 9mm spacers
4 vintage brown 9mm faceted crystal rounds	2 sterling silver 2mm x 3mm crimp beads
4 pava 11mm x 9mm to 9mm x 10mm shells	20mm round silver nickel button* 26" flexible wire
2 stone 7mm x 16mm nuggets	*Available through Rio Grande
2 stone 14mm rounds	
2 olivine aurora borealis 8mm faceted crystal rounds	**Toolbox**
	Wire cutters
	Flat nose or chain nose pliers

round silver nickel button

malachite round

wood barrel bead

round faceted crystal

stone nugget

olivine crystal

pewter spacer

round stone

vintage pearl

green lampwork round

ameythst round

Bali spacer

lampwork rondelle disc

zigzag
barrel bead

black-
and-white
cowbone tube

ivory
cowbone
carved tube

striped tube

ivory
cowbone
round

African picture
jasper

rondelle
disc

black-
and-white
round

black-
and-white
three-sided
round

African
picture
jasper

African Influence Necklace

Designer: *Susan Ray*

Finished Size: 23½" without clasp
Where to Get It: Specialty bead
shops or catalogs; craft stores
Time to Complete: One afternoon
How Much Will It Cost?
A manicure ($20 to $50)

What You Need
4 black-and-white zigzag
  12mm x 11mm barrels*
4 black-and-white
  cowbone-carved
  24mm x 12mm tubes*
6 black-and-white striped
  25mm to 30mm x 8mm
  to 9mm tubes*
4 ivory cowbone-carved
  25mm x 7mm tubes*
2 ivory cowbone-carved
  8mm x 11mm rounds*
5 African picture jasper
  12mm to 16mm x 16mm
  to 18mm rounds
6 black-and-white
  4mm x 12mm rondelles
2 brown-and-black three-
  sided 9mm rounds*
4 black-and-white
  8mm x 11mm rounds*
2 silver 3mm rounds
2 sterling silver 2mm x 3mm
  crimp beads
Pewter toggle set
28" flexible wire

*Similar beads available through Rio
Grande

Toolbox
Wire cutters
Flat nose pliers

*The dynamic look of this necklace proves that even extraordinarily
simple calligraphy can make a very powerful statement.*

What You Need to Know
   See the instructions and
information outlined in Single-
Strand Basics, pages 23-29.

FYI
●Symbolism has been etched
into the sought-after Tibetan
pre-Buddhist DZI beads. Market
interest in these beads has spawned
makers to imitate their intricate
and complex patterns.

Did you know?
●Contrary to urban legend, trade for beads did not start with the erroneous
story of the Island of Manhattan. Trade beads throughout history encouraged
trade of goods from Africa to Europe. Highly prized today, many look-a-likes
have flooded the market, so beware. Becoming a collector of authentic trade
beads can require years of research and an expert's eye.

Canoes and Paddles Natural Choker

Inspired by the unusual shapes of the red glass beads, the canoes and paddles theme of this piece is also distinguished by the southwest influence of turquoise and includes hand-tooled Bali silver beads.

Tip
● Check for red beads whenever you're shopping. Finding the right red for Christmas-giving can be unnerving during the holiday season when red bead inventories are very low. Red glass beads can add to a project anytime of year.

Designer: *Susan Ray*

Finished Size: 19" without clasp
Where to Get It: Specialty bead shops or catalogs; craft stores
Time to Complete: One hour
How Much Will It Cost?
A movie and popcorn
(less than $20)

What You Need
23mm x 23mm Siam transparent bead
70 turquoise opaque 8/0 seed beads
4 coral 6mm rounds
4 coral 6mm x 7mm barrels
2 coral 9mm x 6mm coins
4 coral 5mm x 7mm rondelle discs
2 coral 5mm-6mm rounds
6 Siam transparent 14mm x 7mm teardrops
2 Siam transparent 14mm x 7mm ovals
4 satin red glass 12mm x 10mm ovals
2 Bali sterling silver 11mm rounds*
2 red opaque glass 18mm rounded triangles
6 silver 3mm spacers
2 sterling silver 2mm x 3mm crimp beads
Sterling silver swirl toggle**
23" flexible wire
*Available through Fire Mountain Gems
**Available through Rio Grande

Toolbox
Wire cutters
Flat nose chain nose pliers

What You Need to Know
See the instructions and information outlined in Single-Strand Basics, pages 23-29.

Labels (right): swirl toggle clasp; coral round; Siam teardrop; coral barrel; coral round; Siam oval; coral rondelle disc; red satin glass oval; Bali silver round; rounded triangle; Siam transparent focal bead

button
closure

sterling
silver
round

chevron
bead

lapis
cube

burnt
sienna
seed
bead

ecru seed
bead

Welcome Spirit Necklaces

Hop, Skip and Jump Choker

Designer: *Sol Hernandez*

Finished Size: 17½" without clasp
Where to Get It: Craft stores
Time to Complete: One hour
How Much Will It Cost?
A movie and popcorn
(less than $20)

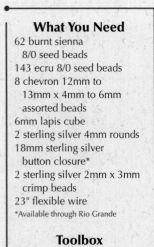

What You Need
62 burnt sienna
   8/0 seed beads
143 ecru 8/0 seed beads
8 chevron 12mm to
   13mm x 4mm to 6mm
   assorted beads
6mm lapis cube
2 sterling silver 4mm rounds
18mm sterling silver
   button closure*
2 sterling silver 2mm x 3mm
   crimp beads
23" flexible wire
*Available through Rio Grande

Toolbox
Wire cutters
Flat nose pliers

What You Need to Know

   See the instructions and
information outlined in Single-
Strand Basics, pages 23-29, and
Button-and-Loop Closures
section, page 34.

These pieces make masterful use of tiny seed beads—extraordinarily delicate, but complex in design. The color change in the 8/0 seed beads plays an intricate role in emphasizing the detail of the dark red and brown trade beads.

Tip

●Spacers often refer to metal beads that separate other beads in your design, although spacers can actually be made of other materials as well. Metal beads are available in a large variety of metals: silver, bronze, pewter, gold and other base metals. To get an antique look, vendors add a patina to the metal, which highlights intricate details. To lessen the expense, you can use base metal spacers colored to resemble silver, pewter and gold. Halcraft and Blue Moon have a large, inexpensive assortment.

Copper and Turquoise Choker

Designer: *Leigh Meyer*

Finished Size: 21½" without clasp
Where to Get It: Craft stores; on the Web
Time to Complete: One afternoon
How Much Will It Cost? A movie and popcorn (less than $20)

What You Need

86 white-and-tan 6/0 seed beads	19 peridot matte 11/0 seed beads
4 light brown cat's-eye 5mm rounds	25 teal matte 11/0 seed beads
2 silver-lined yellow 6/0 seed beads	9 ecru matte 11/0 seed beads
20 copper/gold matte	22 green matte 11/0 seed beads
6/0 seed beads	9 amethyst matte 11/0 seed beads
9 ecru glass 5mm x 7mm abacus	25 brown matte 11/0 seed beads
2 amber glass 5mm x 7mm abacus	13 smoke matte 11/0 seed beads
4 sienna brown glass	8 coral red 11/0 seed beads
9mm x 7mm barrels	2 gold 2mm x 3mm crimp beads
2 sienna glass 5mm x 9mm bow ties	Copper split ring
2 wood 7mm rounds	Copper lobster claw clasp
2 carnelian glass 6mm rounds	25" flexible wire
2 antique turquoise 5mm rounds	
4 copper 4mm rounds	**Toolbox**
83 russet 11/0 seed beads	Wire cutters
13 amber matte 11/0 seed beads	Flat nose or chain nose pliers

---

What You Need to Know

See the instructions and information outlined in Single-Strand Basics, pages 23-29, and Button-and-Loop Closures section, page 34.

Tip

● Adjust your design to accommodate the loop, or your design will not be centered.

copper split ring
cat's-eye round
silver-lined yellow seed bead
copper/gold matte seed bead
ecru glass abacus
amber glass abacus
sienna brown barrel
sienna glass bow tie
wood round
carnelian round
turquoise round
copper round
ecru glass abacus

Words of Inspiration

Beading your own jewelry is such a fun and easy way to flaunt your artistic talent. I hope you enjoy it as much as I do.

—Leigh Meyer

River Camp Natural Choker and Cross Necklaces

Designer: *Susan Ray*

River Camp Cross Necklace
Finished Size:
18½" without clasp
Where to Get It: Specialty bead shops or catalogs; on the Web
Time to Complete:
One afternoon
How Much Will It Cost?
A movie and popcorn (less than $20)

What You Need to Know

See the instructions and information outlined in Single-Strand Basics, pages 23-29.

When wrapping sterling wire to form a secure tie for an object you wish to string, as with the cross on the first necklace, start by creating a loop one-third larger than the bead requires. Then, place the loop around the object and turn it into a simple figure eight. Twist, creating a hanger for the bead. Make sure the wire is tightly wrapped about the bead and the upper portion of the figure acts as the hanging wire.

Silver toggle — amber transparent seed bead — carnelian round — black lace agate crow — black lace agate barrel — black lace agate crow — Bali spacer — yellow jade rectangle — orange round — Bali barrel — wood cross pendant

The colors chosen for this pair of necklaces bring back memories of a verdant nature walk. The choice of beads in graduated size from small in back to large in front focuses attention on the center-front and pendant.

What You Need

4 amber transparent 6/0 seed beads
160 mahogany opaque 11/0 seed beads
26 lime green 11/0 seed beads
6 carnelian 6mm rounds
2 black lace agate 4mm x 6mm crows*
2 black lace agate 7mm x 10mm crows*
2 black lace agate 11mm x 9mm barrels*
2 Bali sterling silver 7mm spacers**
2 Bali sterling silver 6mm x 7mm barrels**
2 yellow jade 5mm rounds
2 clear/orange 3mm rounds

2 yellow jade 17mm x 13mm faceted rectangles
Mahogany wood cross pendant
2 sterling silver 2mm x 3mm crimp beads
Silver toggle set
Sterling silver wire for wrap or 6mm split ring
23" flexible wire
*Available through Crystal Cottage Studio
**Available through Fire Mountain Gems

Toolbox
Wire cutters
Flat nose pliers
Round nose pliers

What You Need to Know

See the instructions and information outlined in Single-Strand Basics, pages 23-29.

Tip

● When designing, do not only consider how necklaces lie on your neck. Each bead must be considered carefully as to where on the woman's upper body it lands. Think about the curves of the clavicle and the cleavage of the breast to determine a desirable length.

River Camp Choker

Finished Size: 21" without clasp
Where to Get It: Specialty bead shops or catalogs; on the Web
Time to Complete:
One afternoon
How Much Will It Cost?
A movie and popcorn
(less than $20)

What You Need
23mm x 9mm red
   lace agate rectangle
6 amber transparent
   6/0 seed beads
112 mahogany opaque
   11/0 seed beads
60 copper shiny
   13/0 seed beads
4 yellow jade 5mm rounds
6 green jade 5mm rounds
4 green transparent
   12mm x 5mm barrels
4 bloodstone
   7mm x 9mm triangles
4 Bali sterling silver
   7mm spacers**
2 crazy lace agate
   19mm x 15mm ovals*
2 picture jasper 4mm rounds*
2 amber 6mm rounds
6 picture jasper 6mm rounds*
2 sterling silver 2mm x 3mm
   crimp beads
Silver toggle set
25" flexible wire
*Available through Crystal Cottage Studio
** Available through Fire Mountain Gems

Toolbox
Wire cutters
Flat nose pliers
Round nose pliers

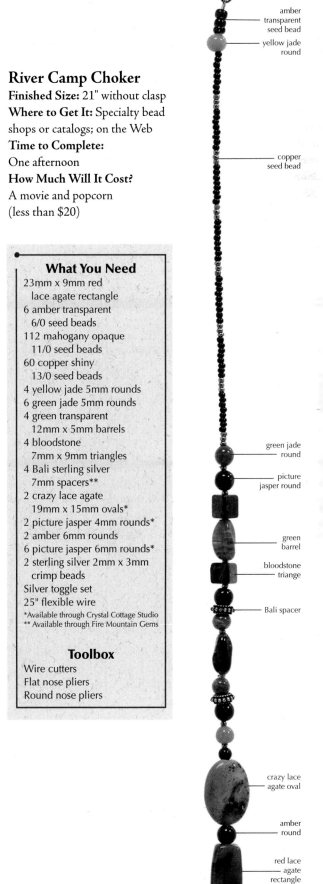

amber
transparent
seed bead

yellow jade
round

copper
seed bead

green jade
round

picture
jasper round

green
barrel

bloodstone
triange

Bali spacer

crazy lace
agate oval

amber
round

red lace
agate
rectangle

Summer Days Anklets

Beach House Memories Anklet

Designer: *Christen Stretch*

Finished Size: 10¾" without clasp
Where to Get It: Specialty bead shops or catalogs; craft stores
Time to Complete: One weekend
How Much Will It Cost? A movie and popcorn (less than $20)

lobster clasp

golden jade cylinder

mother-of-pearl chip

golden jade chip

silver bail

golden jade whale

What You Need
10 golden jade
   8mm x 6mm cylinders
3" sterling silver headpin
½"-long golden jade whale
58 mother-of-pearl
   7mm x 5mm chips*
8 golden jade chips
4mm silver bail
Lobster clasp and tab
13" flexible wire
*Available through Fire Mountain Gems

Toolbox
Wire cutters
Flat nose or chain nose pliers
Round nose pliers

Whether you remember the sunlit walk along the beach to pick shells, the glowing colors of azure, green and pink at dusk, or the adventurous peddler parting oysters in search of its pearl, the memories these anklets evoke will last a lifetime.

Tips

●When you aren't sure if you will like your design—string it. Thread a 11/0 or larger seed bead on your wire and tie a small knot, letting the seed bead fall into the center of the knot at the end of the your wire. This small seed bead will act as a stop and prevent other beads from falling off as you string.

●Do not forget to adjust your design to accommodate for the loop or your design will not be centered.

●Measure your anklet first. Add ½" for added comfort around your ankle. Check for proper fit before crimping.

Pool Party Anklet

Designer: *Sue Wilke*

Finished Size: 10½" without clasp
Where to Get It: Specialty bead shops or catalogs; craft stores
Time to Complete: One afternoon
How Much Will It Cost?
A movie and popcorn
(less than $20)

What You Need
12 cobalt blue 6mm bicones
29 blue/purple 8/0 seed beads
6 light blue transparent
   4mm cubes
6 green transparent
   9mm triangle drops
6 clear with rainbow stripes
   16mm x 7mm rectangles
2 sterling silver 2mm x 3mm
   crimp beads
2 silver 1mm spacers
Silver magnetic 6mm x 4mm
   clasp*
15" flexible wire
*Available through Rio Grande

Toolbox
Wire cutters
Flat nose or chain pliers

magnetic clasp
cobalt blue bicone
light blue cube
green triangle drop
clear/rainbow stripe rectangle

My Boathouse Anklet

Designer: *Darien Kaiser*

Finished Size: 9½" without clasp
Where to Get It: Specialty bead shops or catalogs; craft stores
Time to Complete:
One afternoon
How Much Will It Cost?
A movie and popcorn
(less than $20)

What You Need
25 blue rainbow 6/0 seed beads
14 light green rainbow
   6/0 seed beads
14 dark green rainbow
   6/0 seed beads
4 clear/silver-lined
   6/0 seed beads
Pearl luster 6/0 seed bead
Gold matte 8/0 seed bead
Gold 3mm round
12 wood 2mm x 8mm
   flat discs
5 pre-drilled 11mm x 7mm
   conch shells
6 snail 7mm x 8mm shells
2 gold 2mm x 3mm
   crimp beads
6 gold 3" headpins
Gold split ring
Gold lobster claw clasp
15" flexible wire

Toolbox
Wire cutters
Flat nose or chain pliers
Needle nose or
   round nose pliers

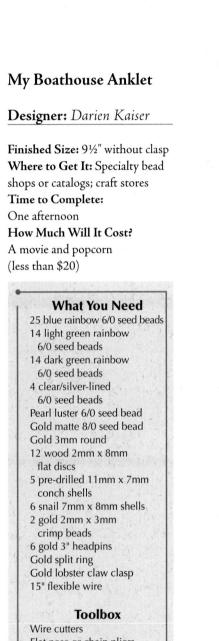
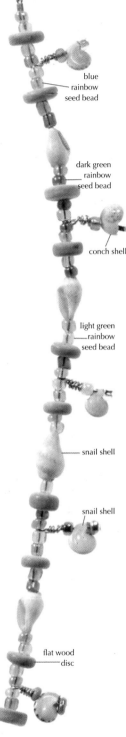

blue rainbow seed bead
dark green rainbow seed bead
conch shell
light green rainbow seed bead
snail shell
snail shell
flat wood disc

What You Need to Know

See the instructions and information outlined in Single-Strand Basics, pages 23-29, and Earring and Dangle Basics, pages 36-40.

The average ankle bracelet is 10" in length (see Jewelry Lengths chart, page 141).

Tiny shells are fun to bead. Be sure to check that their predrilled holes are easy to maneuver before buying by testing with a 6" piece of flexible wire.

On the Pool Party Anklet, note that magnetic clasps work well on only lightweight necklaces, bracelets and anklets. Take care that the length of the anklet is long enough, or the flexing of your foot will pop open the magnetic clasp.

antique
silver
toggle
clasp

copper matte
seed bead

blue
rainbow
seed bead

blue
borosilicate
lampwork
flat round

Mystic Blue Choker and Bracelet

Designer: *Susan Ray*
Lampwork Artist:
Iris Buchholtz

Choker

Finished Size: 17½" without clasp
Where to Get It: From the artist;
on the Web
Time to Complete:
One afternoon
How Much Will It Cost?
Dinner for two ($50 to $100)

Bracelet

Finished Size: 7½" without clasp
Where to Get It: From the artist;
on the Web
Time to Complete:
One afternoon
How Much Will It Cost?
A manicure ($20 to $50)

What You Need to Know

See the instructions and
information outlined in Single-
Strand Basics, pages 23-29, and
Earring and Dangle Basics,
pages 36-40.

The borosilicate lampwork in these pieces reveals shades of mystical blues swirled with opalescence. It definitely shows a touch of metallurgy, ecology and magic. The more you look at it, the more there is to see— quite a reflection, intriguing and evolving.

What You Need

Necklace
14 blue rainbow 6/0 seed beads
4 green rainbow 6/0 seed beads
11 purple rainbow 6/0 seed beads
9 copper rainbow 6/0 seed beads
107 copper matte 6/0 seed beads
8 blue borosilicate lampwork 5mm
  x 6mm flat rounds
2 sterling silver 2mm x 3mm crimp
  beads
Antique silver toggle set
22" flexible wire

Bracelet
6 blue rainbow 6/0 seed beads
3 green rainbow 6/0 seed beads
7 purple rainbow 6/0 seed beads
4 copper matte 6/0 seed beads
2 blue borosilicate lampwork 6mm
  x 12mm flat rounds
9mm x 15mm blue borosilicate
  lampwork flat round
2 sterling silver 2mm x 3mm crimp
  beads
Antique silver toggle set
12" flexible wire

Toolbox
Wire cutters
Flat nose or chain nose pliers

Lime Tangerine Citrus Cooler Necklace

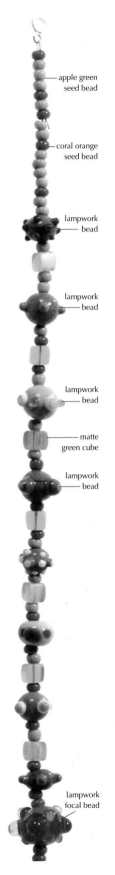

apple green
seed bead

coral orange
seed bead

lampwork
bead

lampwork
bead

lampwork
bead

matte
green cube

lampwork
bead

lampwork
focal bead

Designer: *Sue Wilke*
Lampwork Artist:
Tamara Knight

Finished Size: 17" without clasp
Where to Get It: From the artist;
on the Web
Time to Complete:
One afternoon
How Much Will It Cost?
One-way ticket to London
(more than $100)

What You Need

17 lampwork 7mm x 2mm to
  15mm x 12mm beads
48 apple green 6/0 seed beads
29 coral orange 6/0 seed beads
15 matte green aurora borealis
  5mm cubes
2 sterling silver 2mm x 3mm
  crimp beads
6mm silver jump ring
Silver lobster claw clasp
  and tab
21" flexible wire

Toolbox

Wire cutters
Flat nose or chain pliers

---

*You can slurp up sunshine with this lime tangerine citrus cooler
lampwork necklace.*

Tip

● Lampwork artists often sell their lampwork in coordinated sets of six to
eight beads. If your design uses only three or four beads, feel free to make a
matching pair of earrings or an entirely new piece of jewelry.

Did you know?

● Lampworking is an ancient craft kept secret for many centuries by
lampworkers themselves, who passed the art to only favored friends and
family. Today, various books reveal their secrets and make this art accessible
to everyone.

What You Need to Know

See the instructions and
information outlined in Single-
Strand Basics, pages 23-29.

Silver-and-Stripes Cha-Cha Bracelet

Designer: Susan Ray

Finished Size: One size fits all
Where to Get It: Specialty bead shops or catalogs; craft stores
Time to Complete: One weekend
How Much Will It Cost? A movie and popcorn (less than $20)

What You Need
62 burnt sienna 8/0 seed 126 cobalt
  blue opaque 11/0 seed beads
80 light blue luster
  13/0 Miyuki seed beads
80 clear/rainbow transparent
  13/0 seed beads
10 silver opaque 11/0 seed beads
34 copper-lined 8/0 seed beads
4 copper/clear 4mm x 4mm cubes
39 silver 7mm x 1mm bugles
35 light brown pearlized
  7mm rounds
27 clear/dark amber
  Czech 8mm faceted rounds
21 silver twisted 7mm bicones
40 luster/blue transparent 12mm to
  16mm x 6mm to 8mm barrels
156 sterling silver 4" headpins*
Antique silver stretch band,
  three-row cha-cha bracelet
*Available through Rio Grande

Toolbox
Wire cutters
Flat nose or chain nose pliers
Needle nose or rosary pliers

What a delicious way to light up your wrist. The beads dance like wind chimes, as each view creates a unique glimpse of artistic freedom.

Here's How:

1. Lay out your beads and headpins, making sure you have enough beads for consistent repeats on each pin.

2. Assemble each dangle, using the rosary turn technique.

3. Attach each dangle to the cha-cha band either as you go, as shown here, or with split rings individually.

4. The finished piece is fun and easy to wear with its expandable slip-on band.

Detail of the inner row on the band.

Detail of the outer two rows on the band.

What You Need to Know

See the instructions and information outlined in Earring and Dangle Basics, pages 36-40, paying special attention to the subsection talking about cha-cha designs in Other Uses of Dangles, page 40.

This particular cha-cha bracelet has three rows of loops. All dangles were made directly on the loops of the cha-cha bracelet.

Fish Market Ensemble

India bell

glass fish bead

red seed bead

blue crystal round

blue seed bead

silver clasp

Whether your fish market is at Nantucket or on Delancy, this fun fish parade quite possibly would be the catch of the day.

What You Need to Know

See the instructions and information outlined in Single-Strand Basics for the necklace and bracelet, pages 23-29.

See the instructions and information outlined in Earring and Dangle Basics, pages 36-40, but also note the how-to steps here with regard to working the chain into the design. There is actually a blue 13/0 seed bead under each set of India bells to help keep enough space for the bells to move about.

Here's How:

1. Cut 3" piece of chain. Set aside.

2. Thread a fish bead onto the headpin and create the dangle.

3. Attach one fish dangle to an end of a chain piece, using a split ring.

4. Add one silver bell (attached to a split ring) to the other end of chain.

5. Attach French ear wire to chain 1¼" from bells.

6. Repeat for other earring.

Designer: *Christen Stretch*

Necklace
Finished Size: 21" without clasp
Where to Get It: Craft stores
(for each piece)
Time to Complete: One afternoon
(for each piece)
How Much Will It Cost?
A movie and popcorn
(less than $20 for each piece)

What You Need
80 blue 13/0 seed beads
66 red 6/0 seed beads
14 blue 4mm crystal rounds
2 silver-lined 6/0 seed beads
7 glass 20mm x 12mm fish beads*
12 India 6mm bells
2 sterling silver 2mm x 3mm
    crimp beads
Sterling silver spring clasp
    and tab
25" flexible wire

Bracelet
Finished Size: 8" without clasp
27 blue 13/0 seed beads
19 red 6/0 seed beads
4 blue 4mm crystal rounds
5 glass 20mm x 12mm
    fish beads*
2 sterling silver 2mm x 3mm
    crimp beads
Sterling silver spring clasp
    and tab
12" flexible wire

Earrings
Finished Size:
    3½" without ear wires
4 India 6mm bells
Chain link (cut 6" in two)
2 glass 20mm x 12mm fish beads*
2 sterling silver 3" headpins
4 silver 6mm split rings
French coil and ball ear wires
*Available through Halcraft

Toolbox
Wire cutters
Flat nose or chain nose pliers
Needle nose pliers

opal pearl

aventurine chip

Chinese ceramic round

Bali sterling silver tube

Chinese ceramic tube

hollow stars

moonstone round

light green cat's-eye

flat round spacer

Chinese ceramic pear

Mott Street Splash

Designer: *Susan Ray*

Necklace 1

Finished Size: 28" without clasp
Where to Get It: Specialty bead shops or catalogs; on the Web
Time to Complete: One weekend
How Much Will It Cost?
A manicure ($20 to $50)

What You Need
2 sterling silver 10mm hollow stars
2 silver 4mm rounds
6 moonstone 7mm rounds
4 vintage opal 8mm round pearls
6 aventurine chips
4 Chinese ceramic 8mm rounds
4 Chinese ceramic 8mm tubes
6 light green synthetic cat's-eye 5mm rounds
12mm x 10mm Chinese ceramic pear
2 Bali sterling silver 6mm x 3mm tubes*
2 Bali sterling silver 10mm x 3mm tubes*
2 sterling silver 8mm marquise
2 sterling silver 2mm x 5mm flat round spacers
10 white luster 6/0 seed beads
10 gold luster transparent 6/0 seed beads
8 light amber matte 6/0 seed beads
8 amber/black-lined 6/0 seed beads
12 amber luster 6/0 seed beads
4 teal transparent 8/0 seed beads
6 clear/silver 8/0 seed beads
35 brick red opaque 11/0 seed beads
88 black matte 11/0 seed beads
30 copper shiny 13/0 seed beads
23 turquoise rainbow 13/0 seed beads
2 sterling silver 2mm x 3mm crimp beads
Sterling silver spring-ring set
33" flexible wire
*Available through Fire Mountain Gems

Toolbox
Wire cutters
Flat nose or chain nose pliers

The blue-and-green ceramic beads on this combination of necklaces are a new introduction from China that marries easily with faux and real jade.

Tip

•If you plan to sell your jewelry, document everything you can. Include the types of beads, the beads' origins and history, and even the name of the lampwork artists on your price tags. Patrons love this valuable information and it upgrades the jewelry tremendously.

Necklace 2

Finished Size: 22" without clasp
Where to Get It: Specialty bead
shops or catalogs; on the Web
Time to Complete: One weekend
How Much Will It Cost?
A manicure ($20 to $50)

What You Need

18mm x 12mm black
  fire-polished pear
2 hollow copper 12mm x
  10mm six-sided flat rounds
6 Chinese ceramic 8mm rounds
6 black fire-polished
  6mm irregular cubes
2 Chinese ceramic
  8mm x 6mm barrels
44 clear/gold-lined
  6/0 seed beads
6 silver 7mm x 2mm tubes
2 black matte 6/0 seed beads
4 black Czech 4mm x 4mm
  faceted ovals
2 light amethyst 9/0 seed beads
32 burnt sienna 13/0 seed beads
71 black matte 11/0 seed beads
30 turquoise 13/0 seed beads
27 copper matte
  13/0 seed beads
2 sterling silver 2mm x 3mm
  crimp beads
Silver lobster clasp set
26" flexible wire

Toolbox

Wire cutters
Flat nose or chain nose pliers

Did you know?

● Chinese jade is prized for its
deep green color and opacity.
Ancient jade was often carved by
hand, taking hundreds of hours
to do. Today, other materials such
as soapstone and feldspar mimic
jade. Trust your good taste when
picking beads of jade. If the price
seems too high, then verify its
authenticity before buying.

Chinese
ceramic
barrel

Chinese
ceramic
round

black matte
seed bead

silver tube

hollow
copper
six-sided
round

black
faceted
oval

black
fire-polished
cube

black
fire-polished
pear

Bracelet

Finished Size: 7½" without clasp
Where to Get It: Specialty bead
shops or catalogs; on the Web
Time to Complete: One afternoon
How Much Will It Cost?
A movie and popcorn
(less than $20)

What You Need

27 gold 11/0 seed beads
4 blue-and-white fossil
  4mm rounds
5 light green jade 6mm rounds
6mm x 8mm green jade round
6 light green aventurine chips*
2 brown African jasper
  9mm rounds*
3 hand-cut malachite
  8mm rounds*
2 blue-green howlite
  8mm rounds
2 simulated ivory 6mm rounds
9mm x 5mm green jade oval
6mm dark green turquoise
  round
2 sterling silver 2mm x 3mm
  crimp beads
Gold spring-ring and
  tab clasp set
12" flexible wire
*Available through Crystal Cottage tudio

Toolbox

Wire cutters
Flat nose or chain nose pliers

What You Need to Know

See the instructions and
information outlined in Single-
Strand Basics, pages 23-29.

These necklaces are individual
pieces, instead of being strung as
a multi-strand necklace, so they
can be worn separately when
desired to vary the look from
casual to formal.

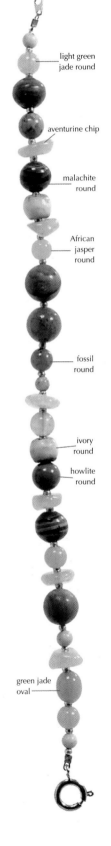

light green
jade round

aventurine chip

malachite
round

African
jasper
round

fossil
round

ivory
round

howlite
round

green jade
oval

Star-Spangled Sailor Necklace

Designer: *Christen Stretch*

Finished Size: 19" without clasp
Where to Get It: Specialty bead shops
or catalogs; craft stores
Time to Complete: One weekend
How Much Will It Cost?
A manicure ($20 to $50)

What You Need to Know

See the instructions and
information outlined in Earring and
Dangle Basics, pages 36-40.

This piece was made on a medium-
weight chain with an antiqued finish.
Many of the dangles were made directly
on the chain. The stars and moon
charms were attached with split rings.

Tip

● Want your charms to hang lower on
your bracelet or necklace? Try attaching
them with jump or split rings to your
jewelry. The rings don't take up much
room and can add up to ½" extra length.
Also consider using tiny lobster claws,
if you wish to remove them for use
intermittently on other pieces of your
favorite jewelry.

*Our fixation with the twinkling lights of the night sky was the inspiration for the
twinkling light of the blue glass, silver and gold twilight dangles of this necklace.*

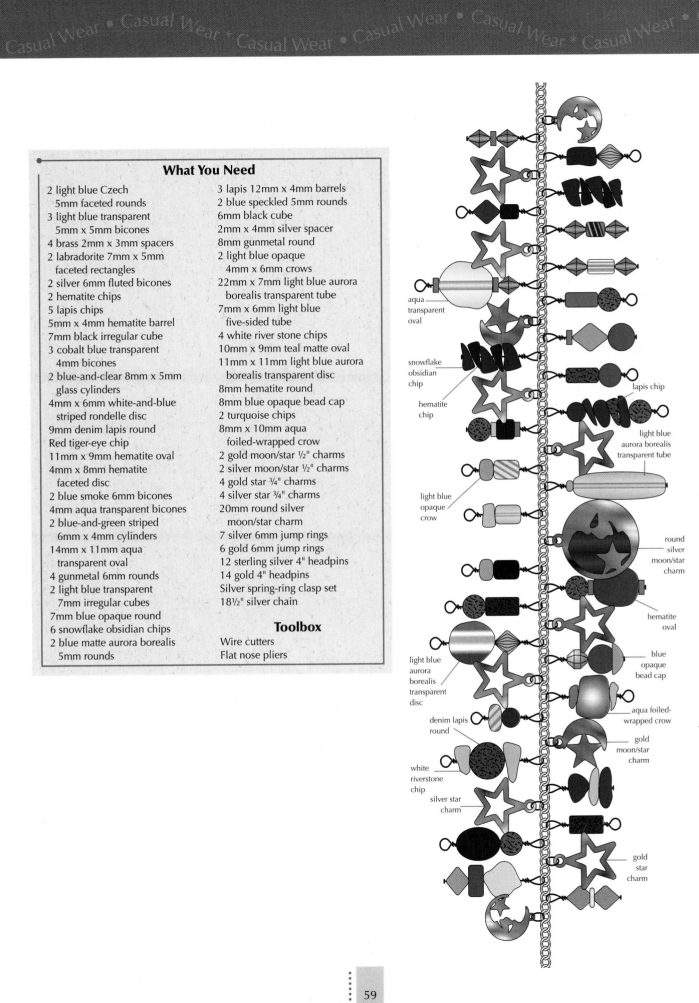

What You Need

2 light blue Czech
5mm faceted rounds
3 light blue transparent
5mm x 5mm bicones
4 brass 2mm x 3mm spacers
2 labradorite 7mm x 5mm
faceted rectangles
2 silver 6mm fluted bicones
2 hematite chips
5 lapis chips
5mm x 4mm hematite barrel
7mm black irregular cube
3 cobalt blue transparent
4mm bicones
2 blue-and-clear 8mm x 5mm
glass cylinders
4mm x 6mm white-and-blue
striped rondelle disc
9mm denim lapis round
Red tiger-eye chip
11mm x 9mm hematite oval
4mm x 8mm hematite
faceted disc
2 blue smoke 6mm bicones
4mm aqua transparent bicones
2 blue-and-green striped
6mm x 4mm cylinders
14mm x 11mm aqua
transparent oval
4 gunmetal 6mm rounds
2 light blue transparent
7mm irregular cubes
7mm blue opaque round
6 snowflake obsidian chips
2 blue matte aurora borealis
5mm rounds

3 lapis 12mm x 4mm barrels
2 blue speckled 5mm rounds
6mm black cube
2mm x 4mm silver spacer
8mm gunmetal round
2 light blue opaque
4mm x 6mm crows
22mm x 7mm light blue aurora
borealis transparent tube
7mm x 6mm light blue
five-sided tube
4 white river stone chips
10mm x 9mm teal matte oval
11mm x 11mm light blue aurora
borealis transparent disc
8mm hematite round
8mm blue opaque bead cap
2 turquoise chips
8mm x 10mm aqua
foiled-wrapped crow
2 gold moon/star ½" charms
2 silver moon/star ½" charms
4 gold star ¾" charms
4 silver star ¾" charms
20mm round silver
moon/star charm
7 silver 6mm jump rings
6 gold 6mm jump rings
12 sterling silver 4" headpins
14 gold 4" headpins
Silver spring-ring clasp set
18½" silver chain

Toolbox

Wire cutters
Flat nose pliers

aqua transparent oval
snowflake obsidian chip
hematite chip
light blue opaque crow
light blue aurora borealis transparent disc
denim lapis round
white riverstone chip
silver star charm
lapis chip
light blue aurora borealis transparent tube
round silver moon/star charm
hematite oval
blue opaque bead cap
aqua foiled-wrapped crow
gold moon/star charm
gold star charm

Spreadsheet Three-Strand Necklace Ensemble

Designer: *Susan Ray*

Necklace

Finished Size: 15" top strand; 16" middle strand; 16¾" bottom strand without clasp

Where to Get It: Specialty bead shops or catalogs; craft stores

Time to Complete: One weekend

How Much Will It Cost? A manicure ($20 to $50)

What You Need

- 2 silver-lined clear 8/0 seed beads
- 30 yellow/gold finish 8/0 seed beads
- 347 gold matte 11/0 seed beads
- 14 silver 5mm x 3mm tubes
- 49 copper matte 6/0 seed beads
- 37 copper-lined clear 8/0 seed beads
- 6 silver 4mm rounds
- 2 silver 8mm bead caps
- 9 silver 3mm x 6mm fluted bicones
- 3 silver 4mm x 7mm bicones
- 5mm x 8mm silver bicone
- 7mm silver fluted round
- 8mm x 6mm silver fluted barrel
- 2 silver 7mm fluted bicones
- 2 silver 12mm x 9mm diamond shapes
- 5mm x 8mm silver rondelle disc
- 7mm x 9mm silver rondelle disc
- 15 Indian agate 8mm rounds
- 12 lemon chrysoprase 7mm rounds
- 13mm x 10mm amber barrel
- 7mm x 10mm moonstone nugget
- 5mm x 9mm citrine rondelle disc
- 6 sterling silver 2mm x 3mm crimp beads
- Silver toggle set
- 19" flexible wire
- 20" flexible wire
- 21" flexible wire

Toolbox

- Wire cutters
- Flat nose or chain nose pliers
- Round nose pliers

Tip

● Beads are like instruments in an orchestra. When deciding on which beads are right for your next design, there are many elements to consider: the shape of the bead; size; texture (smooth or rough); color (cool tones or warm tones); opacity (transparent or opaque); and finish (matte or shiny). Learn to distinguish these six elements and soon you will be on your way to the symphony of design.

Our spreadsheet three-strand necklace, bracelet and earrings embody all that is feminine with lacy edges made by the diversity of semiprecious stones and seed bead fillers.

Bracelet

Finished Size: 6¾" without clasp
Where to Get It: Specialty bead shops or catalogs; craft stores
Time to Complete: One afternoon
How Much Will It Cost? A movie and popcorn (less than $20)

What You Need

4 silver 4mm rounds
24 gold matte 11/0 seed beads
2 copper matte 6/0 seed beads
10 silver 3mm x 6mm
   fluted bicones
14mm x 9mm silver oval
6 Indian agate 8mm rounds
4 lemon chrysoprase
   7mm rounds
2 sterling silver 2mm x 3mm
   crimp beads
Silver toggle set
12" flexible wire

Earrings

Finished Size: 1" without ear wires
Where to Get It: Specialty bead shops or catalogs; craft stores
Time to Complete: One hour
How Much Will It Cost? A movie and popcorn (less than $20)

What You Need

8 gold matte 11/0 seed beads
2 amber transparent
   5mm cubes
2 silver 3mm x 6mm
   fluted bicones
2 Indian agate 8mm rounds
2 lemon chrysoprase
   7mm rounds
4 sterling silver 4" headpins
2 sterling silver French
   ear wires with loop*
*Available through Rio Grande

What You Need to Know

For the necklace: See the instructions and information outlined in Multi-Strand Basics, pages 30-31.

For the bracelet: See the instructions and information outlined in Single-Strand Basics, pages 23-29.

For the earrings: See the instructions and information outlined in Earring and Dangle Basics, pages 36-40.

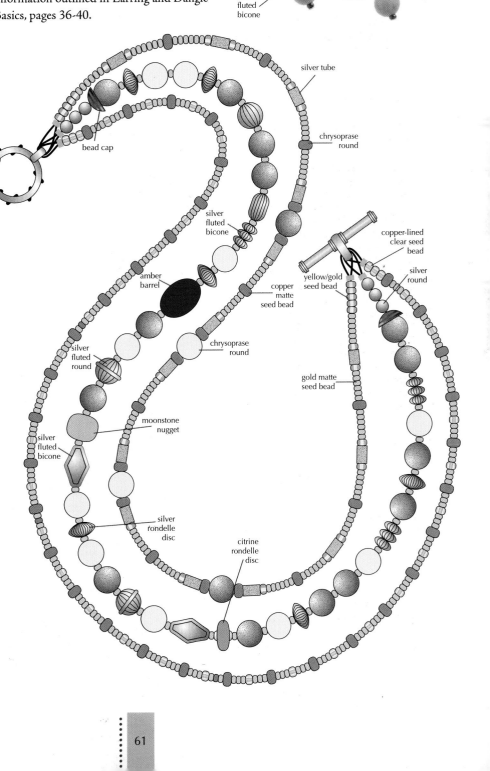

Indian agate round

amber transparent cube

silver fluted bicone

chrysoprase round

silver tube

chrysoprase round

bead cap

silver fluted bicone

amber barrel

silver fluted round

silver fluted bicone

moonstone nugget

silver rondelle disc

chrysoprase round

copper matte seed bead

citrine rondelle disc

copper-lined clear seed bead

silver round

yellow/gold seed bead

gold matte seed bead

Just an Overnight Bag Choker and Earrings

Designer: *Susan Ray*
Lampwork Artist:
  Karen Leonardo

Choker

Finished Size: 17" without clasp
Where to Get It: From the artist;
on the Web
Time to Complete:
One afternoon
How Much Will It Cost?
A manicure ($20 to $50)

What You Need

6 lampwork 8mm x 8mm to
  12mm x 10mm beads
14 press glass aurora borealis
  6mm rounds
7 sterling silver curved tubes*
46 silver 11/0 seed beads
4 sterling silver 3mm rounds
16 silver 6/0 seed beads
18mm silver button-and-loop
  closure*
2 sterling silver 2mm x 3mm
  crimp beads
21" flexible wire
*Available through Rio Grande

Toolbox

Wire cutters
Flat nose or chain nose pliers

A procession of diverse shades of lampwork promenade down this classic choker and the earrings just finish the polished look.

Earrings

Finished Size: 1" without ear wires
Where to Get It: From the artist;
on the Web
Time to Complete: One hour
How Much Will It Cost? A movie
and popcorn (less than $20)

What You Need

2 pressed glass aurora
  borealis 6mm rounds
2 lampwork 12mm x 10mm
  beads
2 silver 11/0 seed beads
4 silver 6/0 seed beads
2 sterling silver 4" headpins
2 sterling silver coil-and-ball
  ear wires

What You Need to Know

For the necklace: See the instructions and information outlined in Button-and-Loop Closures, page 34. When making a button and loop closure, you need to compensate for the additional length of the loop end in relation to the button so that your design will remain centered. In this project, the loop end is strung with only one 3mm round next to the crimp while the button end has three 3mm rounds to compensate.

For the earrings: The instructions and information outlined in Earring and Dangle Basics, pages 36-40.

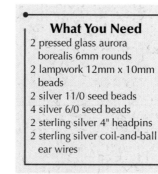

Water Cooler to Client Dinner Duo

The handmade iridescent aqua and turquoise borosilicate lampwork beads shine in this necklace-and-earring set, which easily takes you from daytime office attire to evening fare.

Earrings

Finished Size: 1" without ear wires
Where to Get It: From the artist; on the Web
Time to Complete: One hour
How Much Will It Cost? A movie and popcorn (less than $20)

What You Need
2 lampwork
  10mm x 6mm beads
4 black aurora borealis
  4mm bicones*
10 teal transparent
  11/0 seed beads
4 teal transparent 6/0 seed beads
2 gold 3" headpins
2 gold coil-and-ball ear wires
*Beads by Gutermann

What You Need to Know

For the necklace: See the instructions and information outlined in Single-Strand Basics, pages 23-29.

For the earrings: See the instructions and information outlined in Earring and Dangle Basics, pages 36-40.

Designer: *Susan Ray*
Lampwork Artist:
  Iris Buchholtz

Necklace
Finished Size:
17¾" without clasp
Where to Get It: From the artist; on the Web
Time to Complete:
One afternoon
How Much Will It Cost?
Dinner for two ($50 to $100)

What You Need
9 lampwork 14mm x 8mm to
  19mm x 11mm beads
6 teal transparent
  6/0 seed beads
162 teal transparent
  11/0 seed beads
28 black aurora borealis
  iridescent 4mm faceted
  rounds
8 clear druks 6mm rounds
2 gold 2mm x 3mm
  crimp beads
Gold clasp set
22" wire

Toolbox
Wire cutters
Flat nose or chain nose pliers
Round nose pliers

coil-and-ball
ear wire

teal
seed bead

lampwork
bead

black bicone

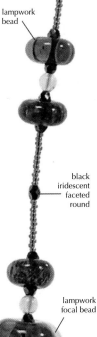

bar end
of toggle
clasp

teal seed
bead

black
faceted
round

clear
druk

lampwork
bead

black
iridescent
faceted
round

lampwork
focal bead

toggle clasp

Botswana agate disc

lace agate round

Botswana agate pear

amber round

mahogany obsidian round

variegated agate barrel

dark amber seed bead

gold medallion

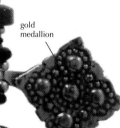

Grande Decaf Mochaccino Necklace

Designer: Susan Ray

Finished Size: 16½" without clasp
Where to Get It: Specialty bead shops or catalogs; on the Web
Time to Complete: One weekend
How Much Will It Cost?
A manicure ($20 to $50)

What You Need
20 gold 6/0 seed beads
44 amber transparent 11/0 seed beads
22 brown transparent 11/0 seed beads
8 Botswana agate 6mm x 9mm discs*
6 black lace agate 10mm faceted rounds*
2 Botswana agate 10mm x 7mm pears*
4 amber 6mm rounds
4 mahogany obsidian 6mm rounds*
4 dark amber transparent 6/0 seed beads
2 variegated agate 27mm x 11mm barrels*
4 gold 6mm x 2mm ribbed spacers
25mm x 25mm gold diamond-shaped medallion
2 gold 2mm x 3mm crimp beads
Gold clasp set
21" flexible wire
*Available through Crystal Cottage Studio

Toolbox
Wire cutters
Flat nose or chain nose pliers
Round nose pliers

No one would ever question your coffee break if it resulted in this delightful office wear necklace.

What You Need to Know

See the instructions and information outlined in Single-Strand Basics, pages 23-29.

Tip

● National bead shows offer grand introductions. One favorite in recent years has been the introduction of faceted pearls and natural beads like these faceted round sardonyx beads on this necklace.

Regular Cinnamon Latte Bracelet

What a yummy way to have cinnamon latte that lasts and lasts. That's what we call jewelry perks!

Designer: *Susan Ray*

Finished Size: 6¼" without clasp
Where to Get It: Specialty bead shops or catalogs; on the Web
Time to Complete: One weekend
How Much Will It Cost?
A manicure ($20 to $50)

What You Need
5 black-and-tan 10mm
   irregular lampwork rounds
4 tiger-eye 8mm rounds
2 amber 11mm x 10mm
   cathedrals
2 hematite 7mm x 9mm
   rondelle discs
2 Bali sterling silver
   9mm x 2mm spacers*
2 Bali sterling silver
   6mm x 6mm bicones
2 antique silver 8mm bell caps
2 antique sterling silver
   7mm x 8mm bicones
4 sterling silver 3mm rounds
2 sterling silver 2mm x 3mm
   crimp beads
Antique silver clasp set
12" flexible wire
*Available through Fire Mountain Gems

Toolbox
Wire cutters
Flat nose or chain nose pliers
Needle nose pliers

What You Need to Know
   See the instructions and information outlined in Single-Strand Basics, pages 23-29.

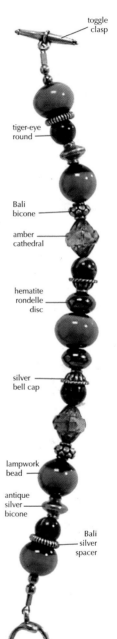

toggle clasp
tiger-eye round
Bali bicone
amber cathedral
hematite rondelle disc
silver bell cap
lampwork bead
antique silver bicone
Bali silver spacer

Tip
● Be sure to avoid using beads that are too large near the sides of your wrist. As with necklaces, consider where on the wrist each bead will lay.

Paper Clips and Push Pins Bracelet

Designer: *Susan Ray*
Lampwork Artist:
Leigh Funk

Finished Size: 6½" without clasp
Where to Get It: From the artist;
on the Web
Time to Complete: One afternoon
How Much Will It Cost? A movie
and popcorn (less than $20)

heart
toggle
clasp

black
matte
seed bead

silver oval
spacer

bull's-eye
lampwork
barrel

spaceship
lampwork
oval

raised
polka-dot
lampwork
round

striped star
lampwork

big dot
lampwork
round

silver
round

What You Need
6 lampwork 15mm x 6mm to
   25mm x 15mm beads
7 antique silver 8mm x 5mm
   oval spacers
3mm silver round
15 black matte 6/0 seed beads
2 sterling silver 2mm x 3mm
   crimp beads
Silver heart toggle clasp*
12" flexible wire
*Available through Halcraft

Toolbox
Wire cutters
Flat nose or chain nose pliers

What You Need to Know
See the instructions and
information outlined in Single-
Strand Basics, pages 23-29.

*If there were ever a talisman to provide smooth sailing through office
politics, it would surely be reaflective of these diverse contemporary
lampwork beads.*

Tip
● Large beads add dimension to a bracelet and will require extra length.
Try it on for the proper fit.

Eating Lunch at My Desk Necklace

Designer: *Sue Wilke*

Finished Size: 18" without clasp
Where to Get It: On the Web
Time to Complete:
One afternoon
How Much Will It Cost?
A manicure ($20 to $50)

What You Need
17 black 4mm rounds
8 black 6mm rounds
60 black opaque 11/0 seed
   beads
21 black 3mm x 7mm discs
8 black 8mm faceted rounds
14 painted 10mm x 10mm
   to 20mm diameter ceramic
   rounds
2 sterling silver 2mm x 3mm
   crimp beads
Silver clasp
2 silver 6mm split rings
22" flexible wire

Toolbox
Wire cutters
Flat nose or chain nose pliers

What You Need to Know
   See the instructions and
information outlined in Single-
Strand Basics, pages 23-29.

*Picasso or Pollack might have easily influenced the maker of this
modern ceramic bead necklace.*

Tip
● Dieting? Make a necklace during your lunch hour instead.

Did you know?
● Clay and ceramic beads can be found in Europe or as far away as Peru. Some
clay beads are carved or painted and fired to a wonderful bright, shiny surface.

silver clasp

black
round

black
faceted
round

black
round

zigzag
painted
ceramic
round

polka dot
painted
ceramic
round

dotted
painted
ceramic
round

purple
and
black
striped
round

black
disc

green-
and-black
painted
ceramic
round

pink
double
dot
painted
ceramic
round

Year-End Report Dangle Necklace and Earrings

Designer: *Susan Ray*

Necklace

Finished Size: 17" without clasp
Where to Get It: Craft stores
Time to Complete: One weekend
How Much Will It Cost? A movie and popcorn (less than $20)

What You Need

- 112 citrine 6/0 seed beads
- 52 silver 11/0 seed beads
- 8 amber transparent 8mm x 3mm flower discs
- 4 amber transparent 8mm discs
- 10 green transparent 8mm x 3mm flower beads
- 14 pink aurora borealis 6/0 seed beads
- 4 matte gold 10mm flower discs
- 2 matte gold 9mm x 6mm tulip beads
- 4 yellow transparent 9mm x 6mm tulip beads
- 4 matte gold 8mm flower beads
- 4 Czech green transparent 8mm x 4mm bicones
- 8 brown transparent 10mm x 6mm triangles
- 4 orange transparent 8mm x 6mm flat ovals
- 6 yellow cat's-eye 6mm rounds
- 4 green transparent 8mm faceted rounds
- 13 red opaque 6/0 seed beads
- 4 amber transparent 6mm cubes
- 4 yellow transparent 8mm rounds
- 2 gray transparent 8mm flower beads
- 2 orange 14mm x 6mm triangles
- 2 brown transparent flat discs
- 2 blackstone 2mm x 6mm tubes
- 24mm x 4mm gray triangle
- 2 sterling silver 2mm x 3mm crimp beads
- 37 sterling silver 4" headpins*
- Antique silver clasp set
- 21" flexible wire
- *Available through Rio Grande

Toolbox

- Wire cutters
- Flat nose or chain nose pliers
- Round nose pliers

What better way to show that your style is "in the black" than to offset a tailored classic gray suit with the feminine Mediterranean flair of this multi-dangle necklace?

Tip

● When you find a color combination you really enjoyed using, make a 3" pendant using the same beads onto a 4" headpin. Later, when you are stumped for a creative idea, look through these pendants and before you know it, creativity stirs! Collect your pendants on large key rings for handy access.

Earrings

Finished Size: 1" without ear wires
Where to Get It: Craft stores
Time to Complete: One hour
How Much Will It Cost? A movie and popcorn (less than $20)

What You Need

6 citrine 6/0 seed beads
2 purple aurora borealis
   6/0 seed beads
4 red opaque 6/0 seed beads
2 sienna 8/0 seed beads
2 amber transparent 6mm cubes
2 citrine 6mm rounds
2 amber transparent 8mm x 3mm
   flower discs
2 Siam transparent 8mm x 6mm
   triangle drops
2 dark amber Czech
   6mm faceted rounds
6 sterling silver 3" headpins
2 sterling silver French ear wires

What You Need to Know

See the instructions and information outlined in Single-Strand Basics, pages 23-29, and in Earring and Dangle Basics, pages 36-40.

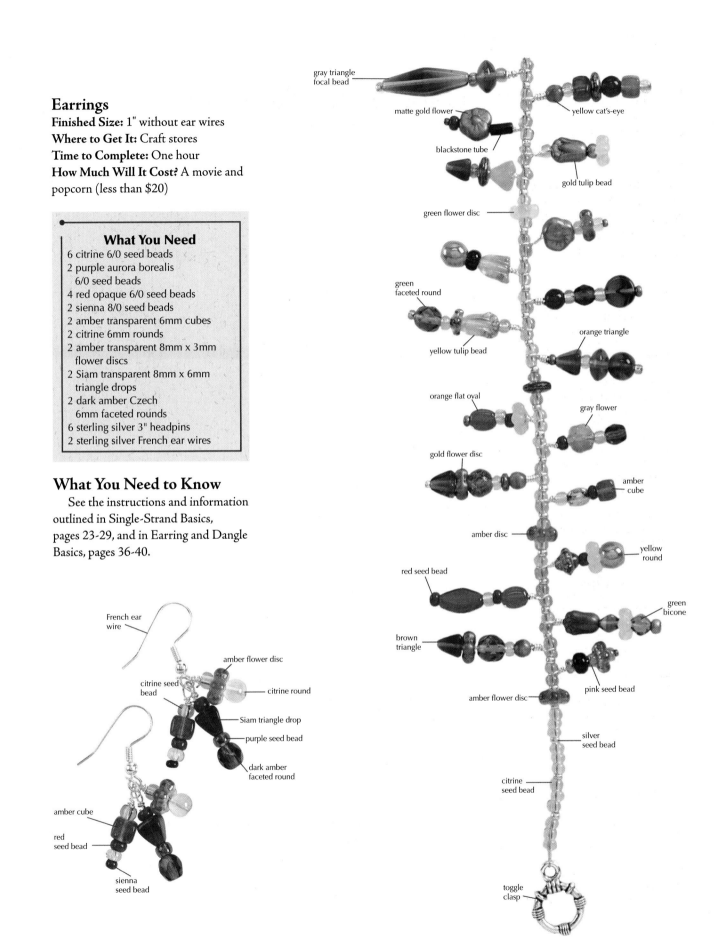

toggle
clasp

antique
turquoise
barrel

clear
crystal
cube

silver
round

crystal
faceted
round

turquoise
nugget

amber
crystal
faceted
round

turquoise
nugget

dichroic
glass
cylinder

turquoise
nugget

Santa Fe Sunrise Necklace

Designer: *Jan Harris*

Finished Size:
18½" without clasp
Where to Get It: Specialty bead
shops or catalogs; craft stores;
from the artist
Time to Complete:
One afternoon
How Much Will It Cost?
A manicure ($20 to $50)

What You Need
6 antique turquoise
  14mm x 5mm barrels
6 clear crystal 7mm cubes
4 corrugated silver
  6mm rounds
22 corrugated silver
  9mm rounds
2 amber 9mm crystal
  faceted rounds
4 crystal 10mm faceted rounds
4 dichroic 10mm x 10mm
  glass cylinders
2 antique turquoise 16mm x
  12mm oval nuggets*
2 antique turquoise 20mm x
  18mm oval nuggets*
24mm x 20mm antique
  turquoise oval nugget*
2 sterling silver 2mm x 3mm
  crimp beads
Silver toggle clasp set
22" flexible wire
*Available through Fire Mountain Gems

Toolbox
Wire cutters
Flat nose or chain nose pliers

What You Need to Know
See the instructions and
information outlined in Single-
Strand Basics, pages 23-29.

Nuggets of ancient turquoise and dichroic accent beads emulate the horizon of a Santa Fe sunrise.

Moroccan Caravan Necklace

Designer: *Susan Ray*

Finished Size: 30" without clasp
Where to Get It: Specialty bead shops or catalogs
Time to Complete: One afternoon
How Much Will It Cost?
A manicure ($20 to $50)

Tactile sense and the earthy tones of this ethnic necklace radiate Mediterranean heat, mystery and intrigue.

What You Need to Know

See the instructions and information outlined in Single-Strand Basics, pages 23-29.

Tip

● Before trying a metal cleaner on vintage jewelry or old dress clips, try a less harsh solvent. Sometimes a mere dish soap and water solution will work just fine. Work in reverse: start with the least abrasive cleaner first. If you must use a strong solvent, then test a small, unseen area before immersing the entire piece.

What You Need
14mm x 20mm wood oval
2 silver 4mm rounds
4 silver 5mm fluted bicones
10 wood 4mm x 5mm barrels
14 wood 5mm x 6mm barrels
2 black 16mm x 14mm twisted horn oval
2 ivory with brass 20mm fluted rounds
2 vintage brass filigree 23mm x 14mm barrels
2 Bali sterling silver 16mm rounds*
2 Bali sterling silver 16mm x 12mm ovals*
2 Bali sterling silver 12mm rounds*
2 carved twisted horn 24mm x 14mm barrels
8 wood 12mm abacuses
6 black 5mm rounds
6 wood 10mm abacuses
4 wood 8mm rounds
2 brown 11mm rounds
26 ivory 3mm rounds
8 hematite 6mm rounds
2 Bali sterling silver 6mm x 8mm crows*
6 black obsidian 12mm x 10mm ovals
2 mop and black 14mm flat discs
4 tortoise transparent 10mm fluted rounds
2 sterling silver 2mm x 3mm crimp beads
Sterling silver toggle
34" flexible wire
*Available through Fire Mountain Gems

Toolbox
Wire cutters
Flat nose or chain nose pliers

silver fluted bicone
wood abacus
black twisted horn oval
carved twisted horn barrel
Bali silver round
vintage brass filigree
black twisted horn oval
wood oval

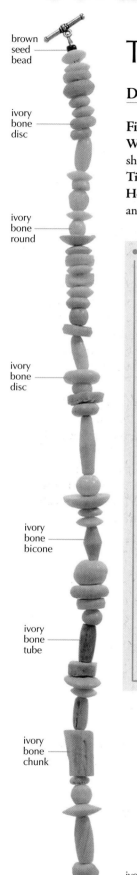

brown
seed
bead

ivory
bone
disc

ivory
bone
round

ivory
bone
disc

ivory
bone
bicone

ivory
bone
tube

ivory
bone
chunk

ivory
bone
pendant

Turtle Island "Tortuga" Necklace

Designer: *Leigh Meyer*

Finished Size: 27" *without clasp*
Where to Get It: Specialty bead shops or catalogs; craft stores
Time to Complete: One afternoon
How Much Will It Cost? A movie and popcorn (less than $20)

What You Need
2 brown 6/0 seed beads
41 ivory bone 11mm discs*
9 ivory bone 10mm rounds*
3 ivory bone ¾" cylinders*
6 ivory bone ½" tubes*
8 ivory bone ¼" chunks*
2 ivory bone ⅞" chunks*
Ivory bone pendant 1¾"
  irregular rectangle*
Ivory bamboo ¾" cylinder*
Ivory bone 18mm rondelle*
Ivory bone 18mm disc*
Ivory bone ½" bicone*
Ivory bone 14mm
  irregular round*
Ivory bone 9mm
  irregular round*
Ivory bone 11mm
  irregular round
Ivory bone ½" bow tie*
2 sterling silver 2mm x 3mm
  crimp beads
Antique silver toggle clasp set
31" flexible wire
*Available through Fire Mountain Gems

Toolbox
Wire cutters
Flat nose or chain nose pliers

A visit to Tortuga will bring you closer to the natural turtles that inhabit the island. Bermuda shorts and Florida wild flower and palm prints are normal attire. This bone necklace celebrates nature and simplicity.

What You Need to Know
See the instructions and information outlined in Single-Strand Basics, pages 23-29.

Did you know?
●Man has a long association with beads. The first beads were likely made of bones, shells, seeds, pods and other natural materials. These beads may have been made or worn to ward off spirits. Most of these beads have been lost through decay. Our love for adornment is left in its wake.

Tip
●Because bone, coral, turquoise and any natural or organic stones usually are porous, solvents can harm the surface of these beads.

French Quarter Necklace and Earrings

Unbridled gaiety and merriment adorn this multi-dangle necklace with matching earrings.

Designer: Susan Ray

Necklace
Finished Size: 30" without clasp
Where to Get It: Specialty bead shops or catalogs; craft stores; on the Web
Time to Complete: One week
How Much Will It Cost?
A manicure ($20 to $50)

Earrings
Finished Size: 2" without ear wires
Where to Get It: Specialty bead shops or catalogs; craft stores; on the Web
Time to Complete: One hour
How Much Will It Cost? A movie and popcorn (less than $20)

What You Need to Know

For the earrings: See the instructions and information outlined in Earring and Dangle Basics, pages 36-40, as well as the swirl-bottom dangle instructions that follow.

For the necklace: Follow the specific instructions that follow.

What You Need

Necklace
192 amber aurora borealis 8/0 seed beads
230 light blue aurora borealis 8/0 seed beads
35 amber 6/0 seed beads
9 fuchsia crackle 6mm rounds
5 amber frosted 8mm rounds
3 amber transparent 7mm rounds
13 green handcarved wood 11mm rounds
3 dark amber 4mm x 4mm cubes
12 orange transparent 3mm x 8mm rondelle discs
4 silver-lined clear 6/0 seed beads
7mm x 7mm silver barrel
6mm blue crackle round

7 orange transparent 5mm rounds
9 amber transparent 5mm x 7mm crows
7mm x 5mm orange transparent barrel
7mm silver round
2 amber transparent 7mm x 5mm barrels
2 amber Czech 6mm faceted rounds
3 green-and-black 6mm rounds
4 cobalt blue transparent 6mm rounds
5mm x 7mm purple transparent crow
5mm x 7mm green transparent crow
2 gold 6/0 seed beads
8mm amber aurora borealis disc
10 orange transparent 11/0 seed beads
5mm x 4mm silver cylinder
15 silver 7mm bells

11 Mardi gras charms (styles/sizes vary)
23 sterling silver 4" headpins
11 silver 8mm jump rings
16 sterling silver 4" eyepins
15 sterling silver coiled wire
4 sterling silver 2mm x 3mm crimp beads
Silver toggle set
11¾" silver chain
2 34" lengths flexible wire

Toolbox
Wire cutters
Flat nose pliers
Round nose pliers

What You Need

Earrings

2 silver-lined clear 11/0 seed beads	2 amber Czech 6mm faceted rounds
2 orange transparent 6/0 seed beads	2 silver Mardi Gras masks
2 moss green 6/0 glass rounds	2 sterling silver 4" wires
4 purple aurora borealis 6/0 seed beads	2 sterling silver French ear wires

Tip

• Lobster claws and toggle clasps can add interest in a contemporary design by placing it to one side, such as the front bottom. This also makes it easier to clasp for older fingers.

Here's How:

Adding a bollo chain: It is easy to add bollo chain to any necklace. Simply use one loop of the bollo chain as a ring, just like with any toggle set.

1. Run flexible wire through the loop and back through crimp bead.

2. Pull taut.

3. Crimp tight.

4. Repeat on the other end.

Making swirl-bottom dangles: When you have 4" sterling headpins, you can create a swirl-eye.

1. Cut away the pin top of the headpin.

2. Begin your swirl by turning a tight half-turn with your round nose pliers.

3. Switch to your flat nose pliers and squeeze the flattened sides of the swirl and then turn, continuing to add more turns to enlarge the swirl. Two to three full swirls generally are enough.

4. Then use the pin with the swirl on the end like you would a regular headpin: thread on beads and turn a loop or rosary turn at the top. The swirls are a nice accent on these dangles, great for earrings or attached to the chain.

Adding on the two-looped seed bead strand: To add the looped second strand of seed beads that add body to this necklace, begin by completing one strand including dangles.

1. Cut a second piece of flexible wire approximately 1½ times the length of the first.

2. Attach one end of flexible wire to the necklace at the clasp, using a crimp bead.

3. String seed beads; string the flexible wire through the pre-strung 6/0 bead on the first strand. Continue for the entire length of the necklace.

4. Crimp to the end of the bollo chain.

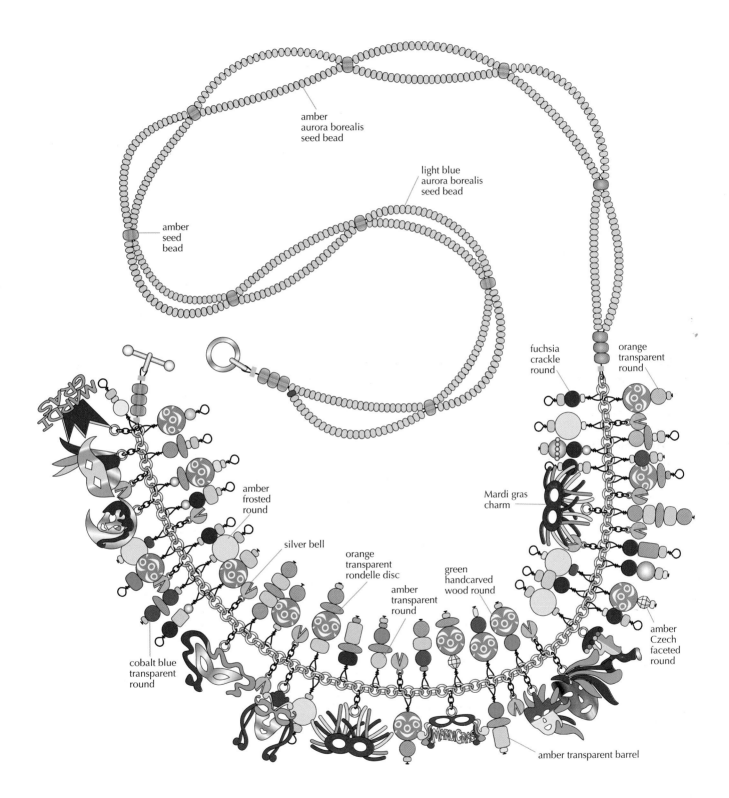

amber
aurora borealis
seed bead

light blue
aurora borealis
seed bead

amber
seed
bead

fuchsia
crackle
round

orange
transparent
round

Mardi gras
charm

amber
frosted
round

silver bell

orange
transparent
rondelle disc

amber
transparent
round

green
handcarved
wood round

amber
Czech
faceted
round

cobalt blue
transparent
round

amber transparent barrel

MARDI GRAS

MARDI GRAS

75

lavender
seed
bead

fluorite
chip

amethyst
chip

amethyst
seed
bead

Mississippi River Callin' Necklace

Designer: *Sue Wilke*

Finished Size: 41¼" without clasp
Where to Get It: Specialty bead shops or catalogs; craft stores
Time to Complete: One afternoon
How Much Will It Cost? A movie and popcorn (less than $20)

What You Need
236 lavender 11/0 seed beads
24 lavender vitrail
  4mm rounds
78 amethyst 8/0 seed beads
18 amethyst 4mm faceted
  crystal rounds
45 fluorite chips
29 amethyst chips
9 amethyst 6mm
  pressed glass discs
2 sterling silver 2mm x 3mm
  crimp beads
Silver toggle set
46" flexible wire

Toolbox
Wire cutters
Flat nose or chain nose pliers

What You Need to Know
See the instructions and information outlined in Single-Strand Basics, pages 23-29.

The murky waters of the mighty Mississippi reveal many treasures. This necklace reflects memories of waters rippling out of cool pools into the current with luscious cool shades of amethyst and jade.

Did you know?
●Amethyst is thought to be the most precious stone of the quartz family. Gem lore suggests it provides love, fertility and a good night's sleep.

●Throughout the centuries, gemstones have been known for mystical attributes. To find out more about the folklore of gemstones, try your favorite online search engine.

I'll Buy Manhattan Necklace and Earrings

You would never trade the beautiful beads of this necklace, even for a trip to the island of Manhattan.

Designer: *Leigh Meyer*

Necklace
Finished Size: 24⅞" without clasp
Where to Get It: Specialty bead shops or catalogs; craft stores
Time to Complete: One afternoon
How Much Will It Cost? A movie and popcorn (less than $20)

Earrings
Finished Size:
⅝" without ear wires
Where to Get It: Specialty bead shops or catalogs; craft stores
Time to Complete: One hour
How Much Will It Cost? A movie and popcorn (less than $20)

What You Need to Know
For the necklace: See the instructions and information outlined in Single-Strand Basics, pages 23-29.

For the earrings: See the instructions and information outlined in Earring and Dangle Basics, pages 36-40.

Tip
● Ran through the rain? Even Gene Kelly would air dry jewelry by spreading it out on a lint-free surface.

melon heishe barrel

red howlite round

golden-eye agate rondelle disc

hand-cut malachite round

What You Need

Necklace
102 melon heishe
  6mm x 2mm barrels
10 red howlite 8mm rounds
16 golden-eye agate
  12mm rondelle discs
3 hand-cut malachite 4mm rounds
4 hand-cut malachite
  11mm rounds
3 hand-cut malachite
  14mm rounds
2 sterling silver 2mm x 3mm
  crimp beads
Silver hook-and-eye clasp
29" flexible wire

Earrings
2 golden-eye agate
  14mm rondelle discs
4 melon heishe
  6mm x 2mm barrels
2 red howlite 7mm rounds
2 hand-cut green malachite 5mm
  rondelle discs
2 sterling silver 3" headpins
2 sterling silver French ear wires

Toolbox
Wire cutters
Flat nose or chain nose pliers
Round nose pliers

melon heishe barrel

red howlite round

hand-cut malachite rodelle disc

golden-eye agate rondelle disc

chain-extended gold clasp

carnelian barrel

carnelian rectangle

turquoise oval

gold rocaille seed bead

Eastern Voyage Ensemble

Designer:
Mary Beth Sprengelmeyer

Necklace

Finished Size: 16" without clasp
Where to Get It: Specialty bead shops or catalogs; on the Web
Time to Complete: One afternoon
How Much Will It Cost? Dinner for two ($50 to $100)

Bracelet

Finished Size: 6¾" without clasp
Where to Get It: Specialty bead shops or catalogs; on the Web
Time to Complete: One afternoon
How Much Will It Cost?
A manicure ($20 to $50)

Earrings

Finished Size: 1" without ear wires
Where to Get It: Specialty bead shops or catalogs; on the Web
Time to Complete: One hour
How Much Will It Cost? A movie and popcorn (less than $20)

What You Need to Know

For the necklace and bracelet: See the instructions and information outlined in Single-Strand Basics, pages 23-29.

For the earrings: See the instructions and information outlined in Earring and Dangle Basics, pages 36-40.

Tip

● One of our friends keeps her beads stored by color. It really makes finding a bead of the right color easy and quick.

You will never want to wish a bon voyage to the classic beauty of this faux turquoise and hand-cut carnelian rectangles ensemble.

What You Need

Necklace
31 turquoise 8mm x 10mm ovals
8 carnelian 9mm x 8mm barrels
3 carnelian 20mm x 9mm rectangles
22 gold 6/0 rocaille beads
2 gold 2mm x 3mm crimp beads
4" chain-extended gold clasp set
20" flexible wire

2 gold 2mm x 3mm crimp beads
Gold clasp set
12" flexible wire

Earrings
4 turquoise 7mm x 9mm ovals
4 gold beads
2 gold 3" headpins
2 gold French ear wires

Bracelet
10 turquoise 8mm x 10mm ovals
4 carnelian 9mm rounds
20mm x 9mm carnelian rectangle
14 gold 6/0 rocaille beads

Toolbox
Wire cutters
Flat nose or chain nose pliers
Round nose pliers

Asian Attitude Collection

Japan: Bold and big in attitude, just as the symbolic mix of coral and bone.

Designer: *Mary Beth Sprengelmeyer*

Necklace

Finished Size: 23" without clasp
Where to Get It: Specialty bead shops or catalogs; craft stores
Time to Complete: One afternoon
How Much Will It Cost? A manicure ($20 to $50)

Bracelet

Finished Size: 7" without clasp
Where to Get It: Specialty bead shops or catalogs; craft stores
Time to Complete: One afternoon
How Much Will It Cost? A movie and popcorn (less than $20)

Earrings

Finished Size: 1¼" without ear wires
Where to Get It: Specialty bead shops or catalogs; craft stores
Time to Complete: One hour
How Much Will It Cost? A movie and popcorn (less than $20)

What You Need to Know

For the necklace and bracelet: See the instructions and information outlined in Single-Strand Basics, pages 23-29.

For the earrings: See the instructions and information outlined in Earring and Dangle Basics, pages 36-40.

red coral bead

bone-and-black matte disc

rough bead barrel

black rocaille seed bead

What You Need

Necklace
2 off-white bone 10mm x 13mm beads
13 red coral 20mm x 16mm to 10mm x 10mm beads
16 bone-and-black matte 3mm x 7mm discs
60 black shiny 6/0 seed beads
24 off-white bone 3mm x 9mm double discs
4 brass 13mm x 10mm rough-finish beads
4 off-white bone with etching 5mm x 12mm discs
2 sterling silver 2mm x 3mm crimp beads

Sterling silver toggle set
27" flexible wire

Bracelet
7 red coral 7mm x 11mm to 12mm x 10mm beads
2 silver-and-brass 11mm x 6mm rough bead barrels
8 white-and-bone 5mm x 7mm double discs
22 black shiny 6/0 rocaille seed beads
2 sterling silver 2mm x 3mm crimp beads
Sterling silver clasp set
12" flexible wire

Earrings
2 red coral 13mm x 6mm beads
2 black matte 6/0 rocaille beads
2 black shiny 6/0 rocaille beads
2 brass-and-silver 13mm x 7mm decorative spacers
2 sterling silver 3" headpins
2 sterling silver ear wires

Toolbox
Wire cutters
Flat nose or chain nose pliers
Round nose pliers

Planetary Orbits Necklace and Earrings

Designer: *Susan Ray*
Lampwork Artist:
Karen Leonardo

Necklace

Finished Size: 15¾" without clasp
Where to Get It: From the artist
Time to Complete: One afternoon
How Much Will It Cost?
Dinner for two ($50 to $100)

Earrings

Finished Size:
1½" without ear wires
Where to Get It: From the artist
Time to Complete: One hour
How Much Will It Cost?
A movie and popcorn
(less than $20)

What You Need to Know

For the necklace: See the instructions and information outlined in Single-Strand Basics, pages 23-29.

For the earrings: See the instructions and information outlined in Earring and Dangle Basics, pages 36-40.

Revolving spheres of swirled lampwork enliven the clean lines of silver findings.

gray pearlized glass round

yellow pearlized glass snail

blue pearlized glass snail

lampwork disc

clear rainbow seed beed

green pearlized glass snail

crystal faceted olive

gray pearlized glass round

bumpy lampwork round

round lampwork pendant

What You Need

Necklace	Earrings
12 blue 7mm x 12mm to 9mm x 14mm lampwork discs	2 bumpy lampwork 12mm rounds
16mm x 18mm large blue lampwork round pendant	4 clear/silver lined 8/0 rounds
145 clear/silver-lined 8/0 seed beads	4 gray pearlized ball glass 4mm rounds
32 clear rainbow 6/0 seed beads	2 clear 9mm x 6mm crystal faceted olive-shapes
88 gray pearlized glass 4mm rounds	2 sterling silver 4" headpins
8 yellow pearlized glass 6mm snail shapes	2 sterling silver French ear wires
11 green pearlized glass 6mm snail shapes	
6mm gray pearlized glass snail shape	**Toolbox**
12 blue pearlized glass 6mm snail shapes	Wire cutters
2 sterling silver 2mm x 3mm crimp beads	Flat nose or chain nose pliers
20" flexible wire	Round nose pliers

Abstract Light Necklace

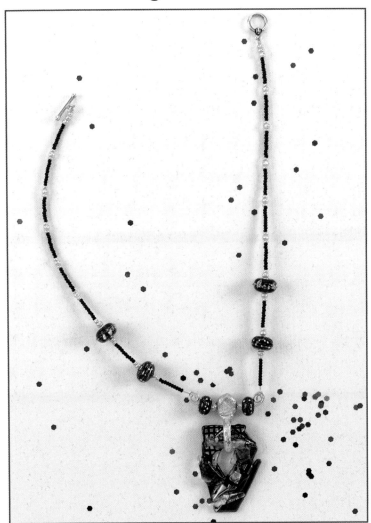

Glowing colors from a fused glass pendant are accentuated by handcrafted silver and coordinating lampwork beads. The only word for this necklace is "stunning."

Designer: *Susan Ray*
Lampwork Artist:
Karen Leonardo

Finished Size: 17½" without clasp
Where to Get It: From the artist
Time to Complete:
One afternoon
How Much Will It Cost?
Dinner for two ($50 to $100)

What You Need to Know

This necklace is a variation to the information and instructions outlined in Single-Strand Basics, pages 23-29. Crimp beads are used on both ends (clasp and pendant) of the wire on each side of the necklace.

Did you know?

● Glass-piled glass wedges melted in a kiln are called "plump" glass as the pieces plump from the heat. The wonderful cabochons by Karen Leonardo are excellent examples of this technique.

● Metal clay gives this dichroic pendant structure and form. This new medium allows its creator to make shapes simply from clay and fire in a kiln. The end result is a .999 sterling form once the binder burns away.

What You Need

2 royal blue-and-silver dichroic lampwork 7mm x 15mm beads
2 dark green-and-gold dichroic lampwork 7mm x 12mm beads
2 dark green-and-silver dichroic lampwork 6mm x 10mm beads
35mm x 50mm multicolored dichroic pendant
Silver coiled focal bead extension*
24 silver 8/0 seed beads
36 silver 6/0 seed beads
160 black 11/0 seed beads

2 aurora borealis 3mm crow beads
12mm silver toggle
4 sterling silver 2mm x 3mm crimp beads
2 12" lengths flexible wire

*Karen Leonardo handmade this spectacular precious metal extension for her cabochon pendant.

Toolbox

Wire cutters
Flat nose or chain nose pliers

---

black seed bead

silver seed bead

silver seed bead

dichroic lampwork bead

dichroic pendant

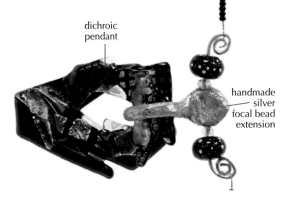

handmade silver focal bead extension

Solo in Soho Necklace and Earrings

black
seed
bead

lime
seed
bead

cobalt
seed
bead

green
glass
round

black
disc

lampwork
disc

lampwork
round
focal
bead

Designer: *Sue Wilke*
Lampwork Artist:
Tamara Knight

Necklace
Finished Size:
22½" without clasps
Where to Get It: From the artist
Time to Complete:
One afternoon
How Much Will It Cost?
Dinner for two ($50 to $100)

Earrings
Finished Size:
1" without ear wires
Where to Get It: From the artist
Time to Complete: One hour
How Much Will It Cost?
A manicure ($20 to $50)

What You Need to Know
For the necklace: See the instructions and information outlined in Single-Strand Basics, pages 23-29.

For the earrings: See the instructions and information outlined in Earring and Dangle Basics, pages 36-40.

Armed with canvas and paint, you can create a true masterpiece inspired by this modern one-of-a-kind necklace and earring set.

Did you know?
● A starter kit to begin lampworking ranges from $100 to $500. Simple multipurpose torches can produce enough heat to melt different types of glass. When the beads are finished, a ceramic fiber-insulated blanket or kiln is used for slowing down the cooling time and allows the beads to anneal properly, which reduces cracking.

Tip
● Looking for lampwork bead supplies? Top suppliers include: Frantz Art Glass and Supply (www.frantzbead.com) and Arrow Springs Manufacturers (www.arrowsprings.com).

What You Need

Necklace
8 lampwork 12mm round discs
23 black shiny 6/0 seed beads
27 lime green 6/0 seed beads
73 cobalt blue matte
  6/0 seed beads
14 green 6mm glass rounds
4 green 8mm rounds
15 black 8mm discs
2 sterling silver 2mm x 3mm
  crimp beads
Sterling silver-and-black onyx
  toggle set*
27" flexible wire
*Available through Rio Grande

Earrings
2 lampwork 12mm round discs
2 black shiny 8/0 seed beads
4 lime green 8/0 seed beads
4 cobalt blue matte 8/0 seed beads
4 black 8mm discs
2 sterling silver 3" headpins
2 sterling silver French ear wires

Toolbox
Wire cutters
Flat nose or chain nose pliers
Round nose pliers

Parisian Salon Necklace and Earrings

Splashes of salmon, caramel, raspberry and metallic blue in the handmade borosilicate lampwork and Czech glass beads make this artist canvas sparkle at any salon opening.

Designer: *Susan Ray*
Lampwork Artist:
Iris Buchholtz

Necklace

Finished Size: 31" bottom strand and 29½" top strand without clasp
Where to Get It: Specialty bead shops or catalogs
Time to Complete: One week
How Much Will It Cost?
One-way ticket to London (more than $100)

Earrings

Finished Size: 1¼"
Where to Get It: Specialty bead shops or catalogs
Time to Complete: One afternoon
How Much Will It Cost?
A manicure ($20 to $50)

What You Need to Know

For the necklace: See the instructions and information outlined in Multi-Strand Basics, pages 30-31.

For the earrings: See the instructions and information outlined in Earring and Dangle Basics, pages 36-40.

heart toggle clasp
blue translucent round
fushia translucent seed bead
orange/pink rainbow seed bead
silver fancy cone
Bali silver round
jasper round
amber glass crow
lampwork disc
purple crow
red glass crow
metallic pink seed bead
blue translucent disc
bead cap

What You Need

Necklace
11 lampwork "ruby kiss" discs
4 silver 8/0 seed beads
213 Siam red 11/0 seed beads
204 metallic pink 11/0 seed beads
153 translucent pink 11/0 seed beads
56 orange/pink rainbow 6/0 rounds
48 fuchsia translucent 6/0 seed beads
26 amber glass 6mm crows
22 Siam red glass 6mm crows
8 purple glass 6mm crows
16 blue translucent 5mm rounds
22 blue translucent 8mm discs
7mm blue round
14 brown opaque jasper 7mm rounds

15 Bali sterling silver 8mm rounds
8 silver bead caps
2 silver 11mm ribbed rounds
2 sterling silver fancy 1" 8mm x 2mm cones
Sterling silver heart toggle*
10 sterling silver 2mm x 3mm crimp beads
2 silver 6mm split rings
*Available from Halcraft

Dangle Hanging from Toggle
11/0 translucent pink seed bead
2 metallic pink 11/0 seed beads
6/0 orange-and-pink rainbow seed bead
5mm blue translucent round

Earrings
4 Siam red 11/0 seed beads
12 metallic pink 11/0 seed beads
4 translucent pink 11/0 seed beads
2 silver 8/0 seed beads
2 blue translucent 5mm rounds
4 orange/pink rainbow 8/0 seed beads
2 fuchsia transparent 8/0 seed beads
4 brown opaque 7mm rounds
2 silver ribbed 11mm rounds
6 sterling silver 3" headpins
2 sterling silver French ear wires
Toolbox
Wire cutters
Flat nose or chain nose pliers
Round nose pliers

Flaneur Choker

Designer: *Susan Ray*
Lampwork Artist:
Iris Buchholtz

Finished Size:
15½" without clasp
Where to Get It:
From the artist
Time to Complete:
One afternoon
How Much Will It Cost?
A manicure ($20 to $50)

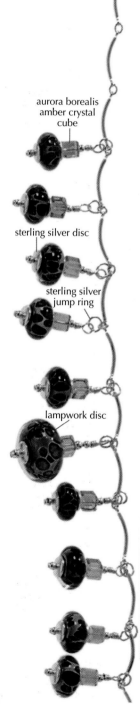

aurora borealis
amber crystal
cube

sterling silver disc

sterling silver
jump ring

lampwork disc

Toulouse-Lautrec found the self-removed attitude of the flaneur interesting to include in his canvases. But there is nothing removed about this delicate choker and earrings with its display of neon blue on soft gold metallic handmade borosilicate lampwork beads.

What You Need

10 blue lampwork
  12mm x 6mm discs
20mm x 10mm blue
  lampwork disc
12 light amber crystal
  aurora borealis
  6mm x 6mm cubes*
2 sterling silver
  4mm rounds
23 sterling silver
  3mm rounds**
23 sterling silver
  7mm discs*
12 sterling silver
  3" headpins
13 sterling silver
  5mm jump rings
5mm sterling silver
  split ring
Sterling silver
  lobster claw clasp
15" sterling silver
  19-link chain***
*Available from Halcraft
**Available from Westrim
***Available from Rio Grande

Toolbox

Wire cutters
Flat nose or
  chain nose pliers
Round nose pliers

What You Need to Know

See the instructions and information outlined in Earring and Dangle Basics, pages 36-40.

Tips

● Looking for more information on lampwork? Try these Web sites:
The Corning Museum (www.cmog.org); The Bead Museum
(www.thebeadmuseum.com); or The International Society of
Glass Beadmakers (www.isgb.org).

● Glass for lampworking is available in rods that are usually 6mm in diameter.
Glass differs when heated, softened, and melted. Some favorite types of glass
used in lampworking are moretti, bull's-eye, borosilicate and shitake.

Byzantine Brushstrokes Necklace and Earrings

The filigree silver sphere and the purple passion borosilicate lampwork beads in deep purple, plum and neon blue inspired the Byzantine link between ancient and modern in this ensemble (featured on the cover, too). Dramatic depth of color and reflective light are revealed.

Designer: *Susan Ray*
Lampwork Artist:
Iris Buchholtz

Necklace
Finished Size: 20" without clasp
Where to Get It: From the artist
Time to Complete: One weekend
How Much Will It Cost?
One-way ticket to London
(more than $100)

Earrings
Finished Size:
1½" without ear wires
Where to Get It: Specialty bead shops or catalogs
Time to Complete: One hour
How Much Will It Cost? A movie and popcorn (less than $20)

What You Need to Know

For the necklace: See the instructions and information outlined in Single-Strand Basics, pages 23-29.

For the earrings: See the instructions and information outlined in Earring and Dangle Basics, pages 36-40.

copper laced hollow round

pearlized round

lampwork bead

copper round

Siam red crow

clear rondelle crystal disc

copper laced hollow round

sterling silver hollow round

What You Need

Necklace
8 sterling silver 3mm rounds
20 gold matte 11/0 seed beads
4 pearlized 6mm rounds
8 Siam red ceramic 6mm rounds
4 copper metallic
   4mm x 3mm hexcuts
8 Siam red transparent
   4mm x 7mm crows
22 copper 4mm x 6mm bicones
2 copper laced 8mm hollow rounds
4 copper laced
   10mm hollow rounds
2 copper 9mm rounds
4 Siam red transparent
   8/0 seed beads
2 copper metallic 6/0 seed beads
24 brick red opaque 8/0 seed beads

11 lampwork 6mm x 14mm beads
5 sterling silver 14mm spacers*
2 copper-and-silver rim
   12mm rounds
10 Siam red transparent
   11/0 seed beads
2 amber transparent 11/0 seed beads
4 sterling silver 10mm bead caps*
2 clear 7mm x 10mm rondelle
   crystal discs
Sterling silver 15mm hollow round*
2 clear-and-copper aurora borealis
   3mm x 5mm rondelle discs
2 sterling silver 2mm x 3mm crimp
   beads
Sterling silver toggle set*
4" sterling silver headpin*

24" flexible wire
*Available through Rio Grande

Earrings
2 Siam red transparent
   8/0 seed beads
2 copper 4mm x 6mm bicones
2 copper metallic 6/0 seed beads
2 copper/silver rim 12mm rounds
2 Siam red ceramic 6mm rounds
2 gold matte 11/0 seed beads
2 sterling silver 4" wires
2 sterling silver ear wires with ball

Toolbox
Wire cutters
Flat nose or chain nose pliers
Round nose pliers

Ancient Artifact Necklace

purple matte seed bead

hematite round

antique gold flower bead

hematite oval

hematite ribbed cone

lampwork disc

purple glass ribbed round

lampwork pendant

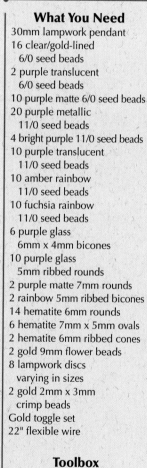

Designer: *Susan Ray*
Lampwork Artist:
Karen Leonardo

Finished Size: 17¾" without clasp
Where to Get It: From the artist
Time to Complete: One weekend
How Much Will It Cost?
Dinner for two ($50 to $100)

What You Need
30mm lampwork pendant
16 clear/gold-lined
    6/0 seed beads
2 purple translucent
    6/0 seed beads
10 purple matte 6/0 seed beads
20 purple metallic
    11/0 seed beads
4 bright purple 11/0 seed beads
10 purple translucent
    11/0 seed beads
10 amber rainbow
    11/0 seed beads
10 fuchsia rainbow
    11/0 seed beads
6 purple glass
    6mm x 4mm bicones
10 purple glass
    5mm ribbed rounds
2 purple matte 7mm rounds
2 rainbow 5mm ribbed bicones
14 hematite 6mm rounds
6 hematite 7mm x 5mm ovals
2 hematite 6mm ribbed cones
2 gold 9mm flower beads
8 lampwork discs
    varying in sizes
2 gold 2mm x 3mm
    crimp beads
Gold toggle set
22" flexible wire

Toolbox
Wire cutters
Flat nose or chain nose pliers
Round wire cutters

A spill of amethyst and hematite match sensibility with the cascading lampwork and the coordinating amulet pendant.

What You Need to Know
See the instructions and information outlined in Single-Strand Basics, pages 23-29.

Did you know?
● For some, the act of melting glass is finite. Many lampwork artists are content to simply make beads and never string them into jewelry. Plenty sell their beads on eBay. Just enter "lampwork" in the search cue for today's auction listings.

Aquatic Exhibition Pendant Necklace

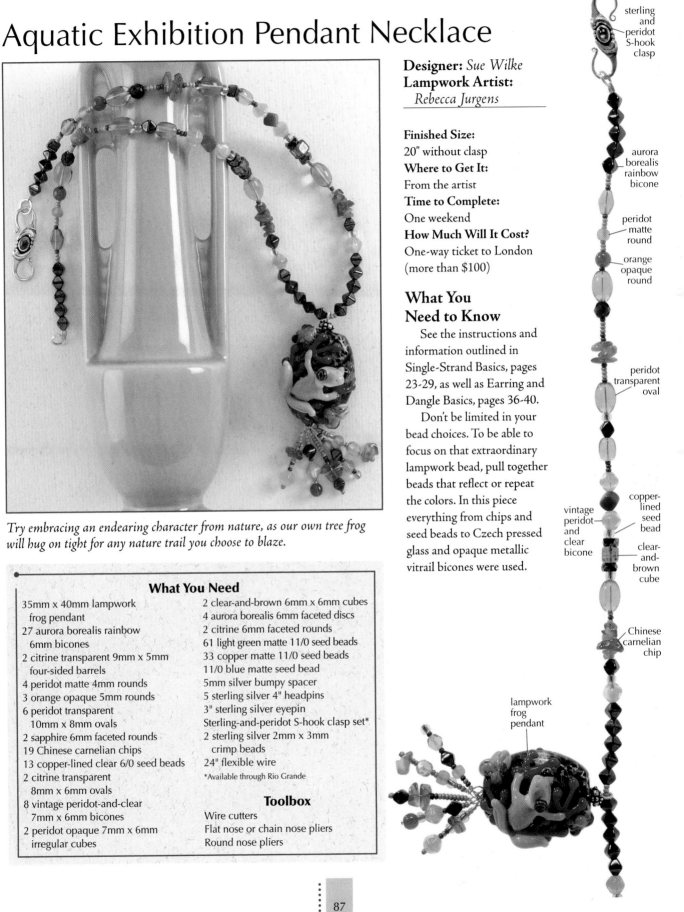

Try embracing an endearing character from nature, as our own tree frog will hug on tight for any nature trail you choose to blaze.

Designer: *Sue Wilke*
Lampwork Artist:
Rebecca Jurgens

Finished Size:
20" without clasp
Where to Get It:
From the artist
Time to Complete:
One weekend
How Much Will It Cost?
One-way ticket to London
(more than $100)

What You Need to Know

See the instructions and information outlined in Single-Strand Basics, pages 23-29, as well as Earring and Dangle Basics, pages 36-40.

Don't be limited in your bead choices. To be able to focus on that extraordinary lampwork bead, pull together beads that reflect or repeat the colors. In this piece everything from chips and seed beads to Czech pressed glass and opaque metallic vitrail bicones were used.

What You Need

35mm x 40mm lampwork frog pendant
27 aurora borealis rainbow 6mm bicones
2 citrine transparent 9mm x 5mm four-sided barrels
4 peridot matte 4mm rounds
3 orange opaque 5mm rounds
6 peridot transparent 10mm x 8mm ovals
2 sapphire 6mm faceted rounds
19 Chinese carnelian chips
13 copper-lined clear 6/0 seed beads
2 citrine transparent 8mm x 6mm ovals
8 vintage peridot-and-clear 7mm x 6mm bicones
2 peridot opaque 7mm x 6mm irregular cubes

2 clear-and-brown 6mm x 6mm cubes
4 aurora borealis 6mm faceted discs
2 citrine 6mm faceted rounds
61 light green matte 11/0 seed beads
33 copper matte 11/0 seed beads
11/0 blue matte seed bead
5mm silver bumpy spacer
5 sterling silver 4" headpins
3" sterling silver eyepin
Sterling-and-peridot S-hook clasp set*
2 sterling silver 2mm x 3mm crimp beads
24" flexible wire
*Available through Rio Grande

Toolbox
Wire cutters
Flat nose or chain nose pliers
Round nose pliers

sterling and peridot S-hook clasp

aurora borealis rainbow bicone

peridot matte round

orange opaque round

peridot transparent oval

copper-lined seed bead

vintage peridot and clear bicone

clear-and-brown cube

Chinese carnelian chip

lampwork frog pendant

Fairies Flower Masterpiece Duo

Designer: *Sue Wilke*
Lampwork Artist:
Roberta Ogborn

Double-Strand Necklace
Finished Size: 17" top strand;
19" bottom strand without clasp
Where to Get It: From the artist
Time to Complete: One weekend
How Much Will It Cost?
One-way ticket to London
(more than $100)

Bracelet
Finished Size: 7½" without clasp
Where to Get It: From the artist
Time to Complete: One hour
How Much Will It Cost?
Dinner for two ($50 to $100)

What You Need to Know
For the necklace: See the
instructions and information
outlined in Multi-Strand Basics,
pages 30-31.
For the bracelet: See the
instructions and information
outlined in Single-Strand Basics,
pages 23-29.

The unimagined beauty of this prized one-of-a-kind lampwork set takes you through a window to a distant fantasy world.

— labels (left-side strand image):
light blue aurora borealis faceted crystal
bright yellow aurora borealis faceted crystal
floral lampwork disc
pink matte tulip
light orchid round
toggle clasp

What You Need

Necklace
25mm x 28mm lampwork
  heart focal bead
10mm x 15mm lampwork bead
4 floral 7mm x 15mm
  lampwork beads
4 lampwork 9mm x 15mm beads
2 floral appliqué 25mm x 15mm
  lampwork pears
12 light pink 4mm x 5mm
  crystal crow shapes
10 pink matte 6mm x 8mm tulips
20 light blue aurora borealis 6mm
  faceted crystal rounds
18 light yellow aurora borealis
  6mm faceted crystal rounds

54 light purple aurora borealis
  4mm rounds
50 light orchid 6/0 seed beads
106 gold-lined clear
  11/0 seed beads
4 sterling silver 2mm x 3mm
  crimp beads
Silver lobster claw clasp-and-tab set
21" flexible wire
23" flexible wire

Bracelet
10mm x 15mm lampwork bead
2 lampwork 9mm x 5mm beads
2 lampwork 6mm x 12mm beads
  with floral appliqué

6 pink matte 6mm x 8mm tulips
4 light blue aurora borealis
  6mm faceted crystal rounds
4 light yellow aurora borealis
  6mm faceted crystal rounds
10 light orchid 4mm rounds
8 light purple aurora borealis
  4mm rounds
16 gold-lined clear 11/0 seed beads
2 sterling silver 2mm x 3mm
  crimp beads
Sterling silver toggle set
12" flexible wire

Toolbox
Wire cutters
Flat nose or chain nose pliers

Pastel Palette Choker

Encased in clear glass, this fresh spring garden will remain in bloom for all time.

Designer: *Susan Ray*
Lampwork Artist:
 Rebecca Jurgens

Finished Size: 18" without clasp
Where to Get It: From the artist
Time to Complete: One afternoon
How Much Will It Cost?
Dinner for two ($50 to $100)

What You Need
20mm-diameter purple-and-white
 floral focal bead
3 oval white pearl 4mm beads
48 pink pearl 11/0 seed beads
72 hot pink 11/0 seed beads
34 silver 7mm twisted bugle beads
72 light pink 13/0 seed beads
2 light purple 6mm discs
3 light pink crystal 4mm bicones
6mm light pink crystal bicone
Silver bail
1½" silver wire
4mm x 6mm silver top bead
3 sterling silver 4" headpins
2 silver 3mm x 2mm spacers
3 silver 2mm x 1mm spacers
2 silver 2mm rounds
2 silver 4mm beads
2 sterling silver 2mm x 3mm crimp
 breads
Silver toggle clasp
23" flexible wire

Toolbox
Wire cutters
Flat nose or chain nose pliers
Round nose pliers

What You Need to Know
See the instructions and information outlined in Single-Strand Basics, pages 23-29, as well as those in Earring and Dangle Basics, pages 36-40.

Tip
● Several companies make interchangeable bead pendants for showing off beads from your lampwork collection. Look in recent issues of bead magazines and bead catalogs to find one you like the best.

Did you know?
● Venice was considered the capital of glass bead makers for centuries. Popular beads made from cane called "millefiori" (a thousand flowers) were created by affixing tiny slices of different canes to a core and winding them over and over in the flame to form a perfectly smooth bead.

sterling toggle

blue-lined clear seed bead

ivory faceted bicone crystal

clear crystal cube

ivory faceted round

clear matte glass oval

light blue druks glass round

Sunday in the Park Trio

Designer:
Krysti Kehl

Choker

Finished Size:
13¾" without clasp
Where to Get It:
Specialty bead shops or catalogs; craft stores
Time to Complete:
One weekend
How Much Will It Cost? A movie and popcorn (less than $20)

Bracelet

Finished Size:
7" without clasp
Where to Get It:
Specialty bead shops or catalogs; craft stores
Time to Complete:
One afternoon
How Much Will It Cost? A movie and popcorn (less than $20)

"Train Wreck" Ring

Finished Size: Size 8
Where to Get It:
Specialty bead shops or catalogs; craft stores
Time to Complete:
One hour
How Much Will It Cost? A movie and popcorn (less than $20)

What You Need to Know

For the choker and bracelet: See the instructions and information outlined in Single-Strand Basics, pages 23-29.

Fried Green Tomatoes
Galena, Illinois

Take a Sunday stroll in this romantic starlight choker ensemble. It's fit for a princess!

What You Need

Necklace
8 light blue 5mm x 8mm druks glass discs
3 ivory aurora borealis 7mm faceted rounds
4 ivory aurora borealis 5mm faceted bicones
2 clear 8mm x 8mm faceted crystal cubes
4 clear aurora borealis 8mm faceted crystal marquise
2 clear aurora borealis 8mm faceted crystal bicones
12 light blue druks 6mm glass rounds
2 clear matte 10mm x 8mm glass ovals
70 blue-lined clear 8/0 seed beads
2 sterling silver 2mm x 3mm crimp beads
Silver toggle set
18" flexible wire

Bracelet
33 blue-lined clear 8/0 seed beads
8 light blue druks 6mm glass rounds
2 clear aurora borealis 6mm faceted crystal cubes
Clear aurora borealis 6mm faceted crystal round

Ivory aurora borealis opaque 7mm faceted round
4 clear transparent/matte 9mm x 8mm ovals
2 sterling silver 2mm x 3mm crimp beads
Silver toggle set
12" flexible wire

Ring
6mm light blue druk glass round
4mm light blue druk glass round
4mm clear aurora borealis glass round
4mm white opaque aurora borealis round
2 clear aurora borealis transparent 4mm cubes
4mm ivory opaque cube
6mm clear faceted crystal round
6/0 light blue transparent round
22" dark blue wire*

*Available through local craft stores

Toolbox
Wire cutters
Flat nose or chain nose pliers
Round nose pliers
Wine cork or small bead bottle

Train Wreck Ring

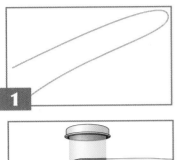

1. Cut 20" of wire and bend wire in half.

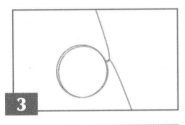

2. Using a wine cork or small bead bottle, wrap the wire around the cork to form a complete circle. For a stronger ring, continue circling object completely to form two loops.

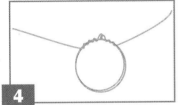

3. Make a full twist where the wire comes together at the base of the loops to secure loops in place.

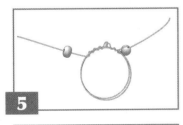

4. Wrap one wire end from front to back through the ring and continue wrapping in the same direction until you have three wraps away from the center. Then, wrap the second wire end from back to front through the ring and continue wrapping away from the center (the wire will be going in the opposite direction of the first wire).

5. String the first bead onto the wire. Continue feeding the wire through the ring in the same direction, but start having the wraps move back toward the center of the ring.

Here's How:

1. Cut 20" of wire and bend wire in half.

2. Using a wine cork or small bead bottle, wrap the wire around the cork to form a complete circle. For a stronger ring, continue circling object completely to form two loops.

3. Make a full twist where the wire comes together at the base of the loops to secure loops in place.

4. Wrap one wire end from front to back through the ring and continue wrapping in the same direction until you have three wraps away from the center. Then, wrap the second wire end from back to front through the ring and continue wrapping away from the center (the wire will be going in the opposite direction of the first wire).

5. String the first bead onto the wire. Continue feeding the wire through the ring in the same direction, but start having the wraps move back toward the center of the ring.

6. String one or two beads onto the wire with each wrap.

7. As you fill in from both sides, see if there are any gaps and fill in with additional beads and wrap.

8. Bring both wires to center, twist to secure, cut excess length of wire off, if necessary, and twist ends of wire into curls using rosary pliers.

Tip

● Black-encased seed beads add drama to this bracelet and necklace, helping to highlight Czech blue, opal and crystal beads.

Finished ring.

clear faceted crystal cube

light blue druks glass round

blue-lined clear seed bead

ivory faceted round

clear oval

clear faceted crystal round

sterling toggle clasp

Ballet on Ice Necklace and Earrings

Designer: *Susan Ray*
Lampwork Artist:
Karen Leonardo

sterling
silver swan
S-hook
clasp

Necklace
Finished Size:
19" without clasp
Where to Get It: Specialty
bead shops or catalogs;
from the artist; on the Web
Time to Complete:
One weekend
How Much Will It Cost?
A manicure ($20 to $50)

pink
matte
seed
bead

Lampwork Earrings
Finished Size:
1¼" without ear wire
Where to Get It: Specialty
bead shops or catalogs;
from the artist; on the Web
Time to Complete:
One afternoon
How Much Will It Cost?
A manicure ($20 to $50)

Dangle Earrings
Finished Size:
1¼" without ear wire
Where to Get It: Specialty
bead shops or catalogs;
craft stores
Time to Complete:
One hour
How Much Will It Cost?
A movie and popcorn
(less than $20)

silver-lined
pink seed bead

vintage
aurora
borealis
faceted
crystal
oblong
bicone

lampwork
pendant

faceted
crystal
round

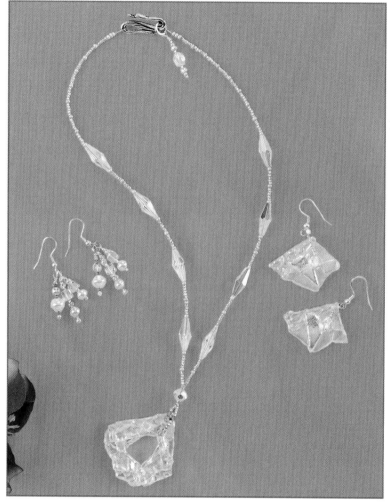

The implied air around this delicate fused glass crystal pendant is enhanced by vintage crystals and foil-lined clear pink-and-matte-pink pearl seed beads. Crystal fused glass cabochons spun into earrings give the ensemble a contemporary flair, while a second pair of earrings featuring pearls and seed bead dangles could be worn for a softer look.

Did you know?
● Earrings can either dress up or dress down your look. Here for the brave and bold, crystal cabochons that match the necklace pendant are spun into earrings with a very contemporary flair. An additional pair of delicate pearl earrings with multiple drops are an alternative for a softer look.

Tip
● Seed beads can provide a refreshing lightness where space is needed in and around a design. The negative space around this pendant and the elements of this necklace are given breadth by the intentional use of the elongated vintage bicone crystals.

Since the opening in this pendant is front-to-back, instead of having a hole drilled side to side, a loop was made for hanging.

Tip
● You can preserve crystals by wrapping each in separate tissue paper before storing.

What You Need

Necklace
1¾" lampwork pendant
8 vintage aurora borealis 17mm x 6mm faceted crystal oblong bicones
2 vintage aurora borealis 7mm faceted crystal rounds
4 gold-lined clear 6/0 seed beads
46 pink matte 8/0 seed beads
89 silver-lined pink 11/0 seed beads
2 silver 6/0 seed beads
4" sterling silver headpin
4 sterling silver 2mm x 3mm crimp beads
Sterling silver S-hook clasp
23" flexible wire

Lampwork Earrings
2 lampwork 1¼" focal beads
4 silver-lined pink 11/0 seed beads
2 clear aurora borealis 7mm faceted crystal rounds
2 sterling silver 4" headpins
2 sterling silver French ear wires

Dangle Earrings
14 silver-lined clear 11/0 seed beads
6 pink-lined orange 11/0 seed beads
2 pink matte 8/0 seed beads
4 silver 6/0 seed beads
2 silver 8/0 seed beads
2 pink transparent aurora borealis 5mm rounds
2 gold-lined clear 6/0 seed beads
4 clear aurora borealis 5mm cubes
4 ivory pearlized 5mm snail shells
2 white pearlized 7mm snail shells
6 sterling silver 3" headpins
2 sterling silver French ear wires

Toolbox
Wire cutters
Flat nose or chain nose pliers
Round nose pliers

What You Need to Know
For the necklace: This piece is a variation of the instructions outlined in Single-Strand Basics, pages 23-29, with special steps for the pendant detailed here.

Here's How:
1. Cut your wire length of 23".

2. Thread on one 6/0 bead, five 11/0 seed beads, one 6/0 bead, five 11/0 seed beads, one 6/0 bead, five 11/0 seed beads, one 6/0 bead and one crimp bead. Slide pendant on.

3. Take wire and go through the first bead in the same direction you went through the first time. The crimp bead should be resting between the first and last 6/0 beads and your wire ends will be going in opposite directions.

4. Pull taut and crimp.

5. Finish stringing following Single-Strand Basics, pages 23-29.

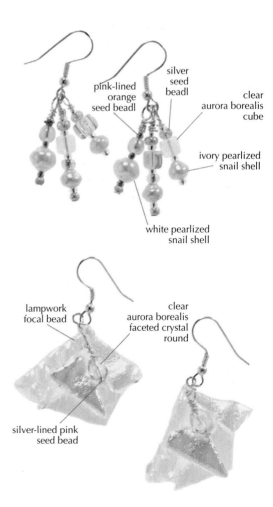

pink-lined orange seed beadl
silver seed beadl
clear aurora borealis cube
ivory pearlized snail shell
white pearlized snail shell

lampwork focal bead
clear aurora borealis faceted crystal round
silver-lined pink seed bead

toggle
clasp

silver
seed
bead

shiny
black
seed
bead

Sold-Out Performance Duo

Designer: *Susan Ray*

Necklace

Finished Size: 16" without clasp
Where to Get It: Specialty bead
shops or catalogs; craft stores
Time to Complete: One afternoon
How Much Will It Cost? A movie
and popcorn (less than $20)

Dangle Earrings

Finished Size:
1¼" without ear wires
Where to Get It: Specialty bead
shops or catalogs; craft stores
Time to Complete: One hour
How Much Will It Cost? A movie
and popcorn (less than $20)

What You Need to Know

For the necklace: See the
instructions and information
outlined in Single-Strand Basics,
pages 23-29.

For the earrings: See the
instructions and information
outlined in Earring and Dangle
Basics, pages 36-40.

This stunning dangle necklace and earrings set will certainly be a sold-out performance.

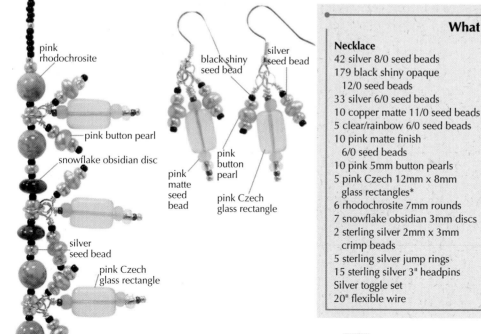

pink
rhodochrosite

pink button pearl

snowflake obsidian disc

silver
seed
bead

pink Czech
glass rectangle

black shiny
seed bead

silver
seed bead

pink
matte
seed
bead

pink
button
pearl

pink Czech
glass rectangle

What You Need

Necklace	Dangle Earrings
42 silver 8/0 seed beads	8 black shiny opaque
179 black shiny opaque	12/0 seed beads
12/0 seed beads	8 silver 6/0 seed beads
33 silver 6/0 seed beads	4 pink matte 6/0 seed beads
10 copper matte 11/0 seed beads	4 copper matte 11/0 seed beads
5 clear/rainbow 6/0 seed beads	2 silver 6/0 seed beads
10 pink matte finish	4 pink 5mm button pearls
6/0 seed beads	2 clear/rainbow 6/0 seed beads
10 pink 5mm button pearls	2 pink 12mm x 8mm
5 pink Czech 12mm x 8mm	glass rectangles*
glass rectangles*	6 sterling silver 3" headpins
6 rhodochrosite 7mm rounds	2 sterling silver French ear wires
7 snowflake obsidian 3mm discs	*Available through Halcraft
2 sterling silver 2mm x 3mm	
crimp beads	**Toolbox**
5 sterling silver jump rings	Wire cutters
15 sterling silver 3" headpins	Flat nose or chain nose pliers
Silver toggle set	Round nose pliers
20" flexible wire	

Children's Recital Necklace

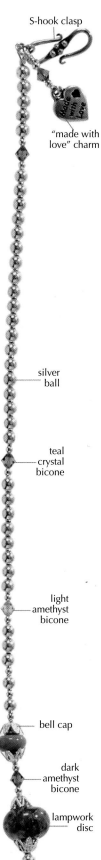

Designer: *Deb Roesly*
Lampwork Artist:
Deb Roesly

Finished Size:
17½" without clasp
Where to Get It: From the artist
Time to Complete:
One afternoon
How Much Will It Cost?
A manicure ($20 to $50)

What You Need to Know

See the instructions and
information outlined in Single-
Strand Basics, pages 23-29, as
well as the information in Earring
and Dangle Basics, pages 36-40.

This necklace has a 4" eyepin
that is used as a basis for the
lampwork bead to become a
pendant. The bottom of the
eyepin holds tiny pink-and-blue
dangles. Strung through the
pendant, the upper portion of the
eyepin is strung with silver and
a tiny pink bicone bead, while
a rosary turn allows it to hang
delicately from the necklace.

A whimsical lavender teddy bear clings tightly to an encased lampwork heart. This is the stuff girls are made of.

Tip

● Simple silver beads are a stylish
element for the basis of this
necklace. Silver has wonderful
reflective properties that highlight
the beautiful lampwork.

What You Need

88 sterling silver 4mm balls	2 sterling silver 3" eyepins
29 sterling silver 2mm balls	2 sterling silver 4" headpins
7 dark amethyst 4mm crystal bicones	Sterling silver "Made with Love" charm
2 light amethyst 4mm crystal bicones	2 sterling silver 2mm x 3mm crimp beads
5 teal 4mm crystal bicones	Silver S-hook clasp set
2 teal 7mm x 4mm lampwork discs	22" flexible wire
2 lampwork 11mm x 7mm discs	
30mm x 38mm lampwork heart with bear pendant	**Toolbox**
9 silver 6mm bell caps	Wire cutters
4mm sterling star spacer	Flat nose or chain nose pliers
	Round nose pliers

(labels on necklace image) S-hook clasp · "made with love" charm · silver ball · teal crystal bicone · light amethyst bicone · bell cap · dark amethyst bicone · lampwork disc

All About Elegance

Matinee and Evening Bracelets

Designers: *Susan Ray and*
Sue Wilke

Matinee Bracelet
Finished Size: 7½" without clasp
Where to Get It: Specialty bead shops
or catalogs; craft stores
Time to Complete: One afternoon
How Much Will It Cost? A movie and
popcorn (less than $20)

Evening Bracelet
Finished Size: 7" without clasp
Where to Get It: Specialty bead shops
or catalogs; craft stores
Time to Complete: One afternoon
How Much Will It Cost? A movie and
popcorn (less than $20)

Tip
● Use only cleaners especially designed for
pearls. Never use jewelry cleaner. Often, a
soft cloth can do the trick (such as a clean,
old undershirt.

*An enclave of silver performs a triple in this captivating three-strand matinee
bracelet. Switch to evening wear as two sets of iridescent pearls and iris matte seed
beads dance around a two-strand bracelet.*

What You Need

Matinee Bracelet
62 silver 11/0 seed beads
23 silver 6/0 seed beads
38 sapphire aurora borealis 3mm x 3mm
    crystal cubes
2 freshwater 6mm pearl rounds*
2 blue freshwater 7mm pearl rounds*
2 purple freshwater 7mm pearl rounds*
2 purple/gray freshwater 7mm x 7mm
    potato pearls*
8 sterling silver 3" eyepins
9" silver chain link*

2" silver cable chain link*
2 sterling silver 6mm jump rings
Sterling silver lobster claw clasp*
2 sterling silver 2mm x 3mm crimp beads
12" flexible wire
*Available through Rio Grande

Evening Bracelet
76 rainbow matte 11/0 seed beads
21 raven's wing purple freshwater
    6mm x 7mm potato pearls*

9 raven's wing purple freshwater
    6mm x 8mm to 6mm x 11 mm potato
    pearls*
4 sterling silver 2mm x 3mm crimp beads
Sterling/gemstone toggle set
2 pieces of blue flexible wire 12" each

Toolbox
Wire cutters
Flat nose pliers or chain nose pliers
Round nose pliers

Evening Bracelet

rainbow matte
seed bead

raven's wing purple
potato pearl

toggle clasp bar

raven's wing purple
potato pearl

toggle clasp ring

Detail of the pearl strands on the Evening Bracelet.

What You Need to Know

For the Matinee Bracelet: See the "Here's How" instructions below.

For the Evening Bracelet: See the instructions and information outlined in Multi-Strand Basics, pages 30-31.

Detail of the strands on the Matinee Bracelet.

Here's How:

1. Cut 12" of wire and knot one end as a stop.

2. String 6/0 beads and sapphire crystals. Knot at the farthest distance of wire and set aside.

3. Cut 7" length of bollo chain and set aside.

4. Cut 1" length of chain and attach to 6mm split ring.

5. Create the first dangle by attaching the loop to the other end of the chain, make a rosary turn, string beads and complete the next turn.

6. Thread second headpin wire (with "pin" detached) to the first and create attachment with next rosary turn. Continue for five dangles.

7. The last dangle is attached to another 1" piece of chain and another split ring. Attach one of the split rings to lobster claw clasp.

8. Attach each end of the 7" chain to each split ring.

9. Cut away the knot from one end of the strung 6/0 and crystal piece.

10. Add crimp bead and thread through split ring and back through crimp and the first two 6/0 beads and then crimp.

11. Cut away excess wire.

12. Repeat steps 9 through 11 for other end of strung beads.

13. To add the tassel to the end of the bracelet, create three different dangles using separate headpins: cut a 1" piece of chain. Make first rosary turn, string beads, thread through the chain, create second rosary turn to attach. Our dangles hang one on each end and one in the middle of this final chain.

Matinee Bracelet

silver chain link
cable chain link
lobster claw clasp
freshwater pearl round
sapphire aurora borealis crystal cube
silver glass seed bead
purple/gray potato pearl

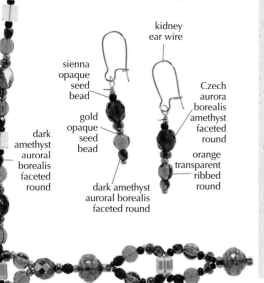

gold
button
clasp

orange
ribbed
round

copper
glass
potato

clear
aurora
borealis
crystal
cube

Czech
aurora
borealis
amethyst
faceted
round

orange
transparent
ribbed
round

dark
amethyst
auroral
borealis
faceted
round

kidney
ear wire

sienna
opaque
seed
bead

gold
opaque
seed
bead

Czech
aurora
borealis
amethyst
faceted
round

orange
transparent
ribbed
round

dark amethyst
auroral borealis
faceted round

Opera at Eight Necklace and Earrings

Designer: *Susan Ray*

Necklace

Finished Size:
30" without clasp
Where to Get It: Craft stores
Time to Complete:
One afternoon
How Much Will It Cost?
A movie and popcorn
(less than $20)

Earrings

Finished Size:
1¼" without ear wires
Where to Get It: Craft stores
Time to Complete: One hour
How Much Will It Cost?
A movie and popcorn
(less than $20)

What You Need to Know

For the necklace: See the instructions and information outlined in Single-Strand Basics, pages 23-29.

For the earrings: See the instructions and information outlined in Earring and Dangle Basics, pages 36-40.

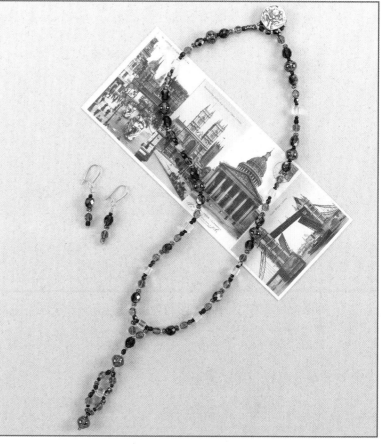

Jewel tones sing with vivid voice in this elegant drop pendant necklace. The house lights reflected in the crystals bring sparkle to the evening.

What You Need

Necklace
32 iris blue 6/0 seed beads
27 gold opaque 8/0 seed beads
8 gold opaque 11/0 seed beads
2 copper matte 11/0 seed beads
36 sienna opaque 8/0 seed beads
6/0 black-lined orange seed bead
35 dark aurora borealis amethyst
 Czech 4mm faceted rounds
17 dark amethyst aurora borealis
 Czech 8mm x 7mm faceted rounds
26 orange transparent
 6mm ribbed rounds
8 copper glass 8mm x 9mm
 potato shapes
10 clear aurora borealis
 6mm crystal cubes*
20mm gold button round
4 gold 2mm crimp beads
Button clasp

48" flexible wire
*Available from Halcraft

Earrings
4 gold opaque 11/0 seed beads
2 gold opaque 8/0 seed beads
2 sienna opaque 8/0 seed beads
2 rainbow blue 6/0 seed beads
2 dark amethyst aurora borealis
 Czech 4mm faceted rounds
2 dark amethyst aurora borealis
 Czech 8mm faceted rounds
2 orange transparent 6mm ribbed rounds
2 gold 4" headpins
2 gold kidney ear wires

Toolbox
Wire cutters
Flat nose or chain nose pliers
Round nose pliers

Turner Hall Box Seats and Balcony Bracelets

Beautiful collections of charms and stones in amber and purple glitter across these show-stopping bracelets. These bracelets work up so quickly that they would be great gifts to give.

Designer: *Jessica Italia*

Box Seats Dangle Bracelet
Finished Size: 7½" without clasp
Where to Get It: Craft stores
Time to Complete: One afternoon
How Much Will It Cost? A manicure ($20 to $50)

Balcony Dangle Bracelet
Finished Size: 7¼" without clasp
Where to Get It: Craft stores
Time to Complete: One afternoon
How Much Will It Cost? A manicure ($20 to $50)

What You Need to Know
See the instructions and information outlined in Earring and Dangle Basics, pages 36-40.

Here's How:
String all of your headpins with beads and set aside. Vary your patterns, but allow for some duplicates. The duplication adds consistency to the design.

1. Starting on one end of the bracelet, insert the headpin (with the beads on) through a link in the chain.

2. Create a rosary turn right onto the twisted cable link of the bracelet.

3. Repeat to finish. You may also use jump rings to add the dangles and charms to the design.

What You Need

Box Seats Dangle Bracelet
3 amber transparent 7mm faceted rounds
3 copper 8mm bicones
3 vintage ivory aurora borealis
   7mm bicones
3 clear glass 13mm x 7mm twist tubes
3 pink transparent aurora borealis
   8mm faceted rounds
3 copper 6mm bicones
3 vintage tan 14mm x 9mm rectangles
3 olivine-and-gold finish
   9mm faceted discs
3 clear rainbow 8mm coins
2 purple glass pearl 9mm rounds
2 vintage olivine crystal
   9mm faceted rounds

2 pink glass pearl 9mm rounds
8mm ivory aurora borealis faceted disc
8 sterling silver 3mm spacers
7¼" copper cable-link 6mm chain
Copper toggle set
34 copper .025" thick/2" long headpins

Balcony Dangle Bracelet
3 light amber Czech fire 6mm faceted
   rounds
3 rose/gold fancy Czech 6mm faceted cubes
3 light amber Czech fire
   8mm faceted rounds
3 pink/peach cats eye 7mm rounds
3 gold ribbed 6mm bicones
3 dark amber 8mm x 5mm bicones

3 hematite 5mm x 3mm barrels
3 beige 5mm rounds
3 dark amber 12mm x 7mm twist barrels
9 gold 4mm spacers
6 gold 19mm x 12mm cross charms
7" gold-plated double-link chain
Gold-plated toggle
11 gold-plated jump rings
27 gold-plated 3" headpins

Toolbox
Wire cutters
Flat nose or chain nose pliers
Round nose pliers

Mistletoe Ball Necklace and Earrings

Designer: *Susan Brusch*

Necklace
Finished Size: 17" without clasp
Where to Get It: Specialty bead shops
or catalogs; craft stores
Time to Complete: One weekend
How Much Will It Cost?
A manicure ($20 to $50)

Earrings
Finished Size: 1¾" without ear wires
Where to Get It: Specialty bead shops
or catalogs; craft stores
Time to Complete: One afternoon
How Much Will It Cost? A movie and
popcorn (less than $20)

What You Need to Know
For the necklace: See the instructions
and information outlined in Single-
Strand Basics, pages 23-29, plus the
additional instruction provided below.

For the earrings: See the instructions
and information outlined in Earring
and Dangle Basics, pages 36-40.

Here's How:
1. Cut your flexible wire 10" longer
than the finished length to compensate
for the interwoven pendant.
2. Divide your wire in half.
3. String on one crimp bead, letting
it fall to the center of your wire. An
alternate way to start this is instead of
using a crimp bead, use a single seed bead
as the beginning, centered on your wire.
4. String both ends of wire together
through the first and second bead.
5. Check to see the wires are still evenly
divided and then flatten the crimp.
6. Separate the wire stands, string
eight beads on each strand.
7. String each wire through one
crystal cube from opposite sides.
8. Once emerged, string eight
additional beads on each side and then
string both wires through a single crimp.

This luminous necklace with beaded drop pendant and button-and-loop closure is ready for all special occasions.

9. Tighten the stringing and flatten
the crimp.
10. String six additional beads onto
both wires, held together as one.
11. Emerge and string five remaining
beads on each wire separately before
ending at another crystal cube.

12. String wires through the cube
from opposite sides and then begin to
string rest of the necklace in place.
13. End with button closure,
referring back to the Button-and-Loop
Closure instructions on page 34 for
assistance, if necessary.

What You Need

Necklace
188 amber translucent 13/0 seed beads
25 amber/black-lined 6/0 seed beads
12 amber 6mm faceted glass,
  varies in size
8 multi with aurora borealis
  6mm faceted rounds
2 clear aurora borealis
  5mm faceted crystal rounds
12mm amber faceted cube
4 gold 4mm bead caps
10mm gold bead cap
8mm gold laced hollow round
3mm gold ball
5 gold 3" headpins
2 sterling silver 2mm x 3mm
  crimp beads

Gold rectangle safety pearl clasp
21" flexible wire

Earrings
2 amber-and-black-lined 6/0 seed beads
4 black-and-gold aurora borealis 6mm
  faceted rounds
2 amber 12mm x 12mm faceted cubes
2 gold 8mm bead caps
2 gold 3" eyepins
2 gold 3" headpins
2 gold French ear wires

Toolbox
Wire cutters
Flat nose or chain nose pliers
Round nose pliers

Bravissimo Necklace

This stunningly elegant necklace showcases a sprinkling of antique jet and fuchsia crystals. Nothing could match its sparkle against the skin of its wearer.

Designer: *Annie Hinton*

Finished Size: Strands are 13"
to 24" in length without clasp
Where to Get It: Craft stores
Time to Complete: One week
How Much Will It Cost?
A manicure ($20 to $50)

What You Need

755 black shiny opaque
  11/0 seed beads
10 black Czech 6mm glass rounds
12 black 5mm glass rounds
6 black 6mm x 6mm glass cubes
3 black 7mm glass stars
2 black 4mm crystal bicones
10 smoke/amethyst-lined
  6mm diamond shapes
4 fuchsia 2mm crystal bicones
26 fuchsia 6mm crystal bicones
3 fuchsia crystal 8mm bicones
29 vintage jet 9mm faceted discs
6 black 12mm faceted rounds
2 fiberglass 7mm x 7mm cubes
2 dark black/amethyst
  20mm x 8mm flat ovals
2 black 12mm x 8mm
  faceted barrels
10 sterling silver 2mm x 3mm
  crimp beads
Vintage silver three-hole hook clasp
5 pieces of wire, 27" each

Toolbox
Wire cutters
Flat nose or chain nose pliers
Round nose pliers

What You Need to Know

See the instructions and information
outlined in Multi-Strand Basics,
pages 30-31.

Tip

● Use of a multi-strand bead board will
make this an easy project. When strung,
measure each strand to your neck.
Measure one completed five-strand for
proper placement. Then crimp.

Wedding Whites Choker

Designer: *Christen Stretch*

Finished Size: 17", will stretch to fit
Where to Get It: Specialty bead shops or catalogs; craft stores
Time to Complete: One weekend
How Much Will It Cost? A movie and popcorn (less than $20)

What You Need to Know

See the instructions and information outlined on pages 25-27 for the closure.

What You Need

4 crème pearl 3mm rounds
198 gold-lined 13/0 seed beads
110 crème pearl 5.5mm rounds
14 vintage clear 6mm x 3mm
  crystal bicones
20 vintage aurora borealis
  7mm x 5mm crystal ovals
12 vintage aurora borealis
  8mm x 6mm crystal ovals
10 vintage aurora borealis
  9mm x 7mm crystal ovals
2 vintage aurora borealis
  10mm x 8mm crystal ovals
4 gold 2mm x 3mm crimp beads
Gold toggle set
2 yards of flexible wire

Toolbox

Wire cutters
Flat nose or chain nose pliers
Round nose pliers

No walk down the aisle would be complete without a lovely choker of pearls and crystals, just like the one shown here.

Did you know?

● Once bead weaving was thought not to work with flexible wire. Now that myth is broken. This entire choker was strung in just one evening on strong flexible wire that actually gives the piece lots of stretch and bounce, too.

Tips

● The necklace is designed for comfort with drops only on the front.
● Customize your wedding by making your own jewelry and jewelry pieces for your wedding party. What a great way to remember a beautiful day!
● The oils from fingertips, perfume and body lotions can dull the surface of crystal jewelry. Wash the surface gently with a mild soap and water.

Here's How:

1. Attach one end of your clasp to the wire by threading the crimp bead onto the wire, threading the wire through the loop of the toggle and the end of wire back through the crimp bead. Using a flat nose pliers, crimp. Repeat for the second wire.

2. Begin to thread beads onto your first wire, following the blue line in the accompanying illustration. Add seven beads to the second wire, as illustrated by the pink line.

3. Thread both wires through the same pearl, as shown in the step 2 illustration. The wires will enter the pearl from opposite directions.

4. Continue in this manner to string three more bead segments.

5. The fifth segment begins the drop pattern, as shown. To create the drops, string through the first two beads on the segment, add a seed bead, bicone crystal and another seed bead (this last seed bead acts as a stop).

6. Avoiding the last seed bead, thread the wire back through the bicone crystal in the opposite direction and continue on, as illustrated.

7. End the piece, as you began.

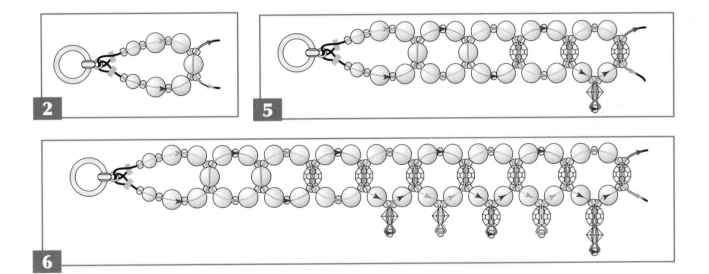

Simply Classic Cabbage Rose Choker and Earrings

Designer: *Jeanne Holland*

Choker

Finished Size: 16" without clasp
Where to Get It: From the artist
Time to Complete: One week
How Much Will It Cost? A manicure ($20 to $50)

Earrings

Finished Size: 2" without earwires
Where to Get It: From the artist
Time to Complete: One hour
How Much Will It Cost? A movie and popcorn (less than $20)

Tip

● Vintaj original art jewelry is designed using an innovative "brass-encased glass" settings concept developed by Wendy Mullane and Jeanne Holland. For information on ordering the vintage filigrees and findings shown in the projects on these pages, see Resources, page 143.

A rose frozen in time is a stunning centerpiece for this Victorian creation. The vintage beads of pink, green and brown beautifully reinforce the sentiment.

What You Need

Necklace

18mm vintage glass "Laliquesque" rose pendant on top of 20mm cameo blush art glass cabochon
18 semiprecious pink-and-black mottled 8mm rounds
4 vintage green-and-brown 7mm art glass rounds
2 vintage speckled 6mm matte glass rounds
2 moss green 10mm art glass rounds
2¼" filigree wrap*
½" filigree clasp*
36 Karmul finish 4mm jump rings*
26 Karmul finish 1" eyepins*
24 Karmul finish 8mm bead caps*
4 Karmul finish 1" muti-end connectors*

Earrings

2 semiprecious pink-and-black mottled 8mm rounds
2 vintage green-and-brown 7mm art glass rounds
6 Karmul finish 8mm bead caps*
2 Karmul finish 1" headpins*
2 Karmul finish 1" eyepins*
2 Karmul finish 4mm jump rings*
2 Karmul finish ear wires*
*Available through Karmul Studios

Toolbox

Wire cutters
Round nose pliers
Flat nose pliers

Here's How to Assemble Multi-Stand Ends:

1. Here are the components you need: beads, eyepins, bead caps, jump rings, and a multi-end connector.

2. Insert eyepin through bead cap, bead and another bead cap. Turn loop on end of eyepin to secure.

3. Attach bead components to connector with jump rings. Close securely.

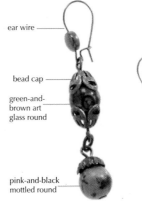

ear wire

bead cap

green-and-brown art glass round

pink-and-black mottled round

Here's How to Assemble an Earring:

1. Connect the beaded portions to one another.

2. Hang the earring on the ear wire.

filigree clasp

bead cap

speckled matte glass round

pink-and-black mottled round

green-and-brown art glass round

multi-end connector

moss green art glass round

filigree wrap

cameo art glass cabochon

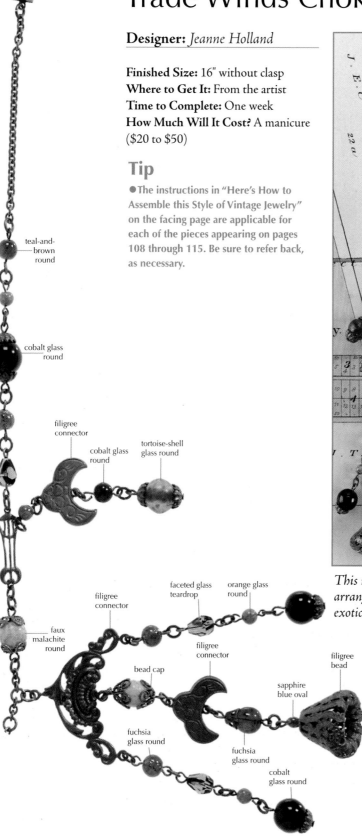

filigree clasp

teal-and-brown round

cobalt glass round

filigree connector

cobalt glass round

tortoise-shell glass round

faux malachite round

filigree connector

faceted glass teardrop

orange glass round

filigree connector

bead cap

fuchsia glass round

filigree bead

fuchsia glass round

sapphire blue oval

cobalt glass round

Trade Winds Choker

Designer: *Jeanne Holland*

Finished Size: 16" without clasp
Where to Get It: From the artist
Time to Complete: One week
How Much Will It Cost? A manicure ($20 to $50)

Tip

●The instructions in "Here's How to Assemble this Style of Vintage Jewelry" on the facing page are applicable for each of the pieces appearing on pages 108 through 115. Be sure to refer back, as necessary.

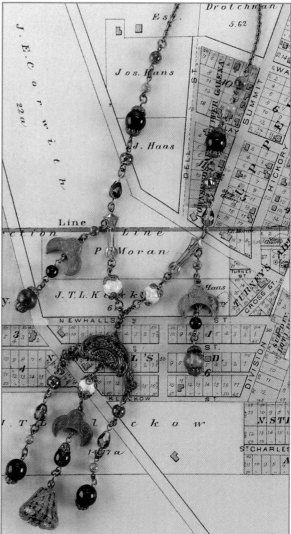

This necklace, with its stunning vintage glass "stones" arranged in drops, truly feels like it sailed in on favored exotic breezes.

What You Need

20mm vintage Karmul finish filigree bead*
2mm sapphire blue opalescent
    flashed-glass oval
4 tortoise-shell 5mm
    faceted glass teardrops
6 vintage orange 4mm
    mottled art glass rounds
2 vintage cobalt 5mm glass rounds
4 vintage cobalt 10mm glass rounds
4 vintage fuchsia foil art
    5mm glass rounds

7mm vintage fuchsia-and-black
    art glass round
2 teal-and-brown 5mm
    mottled art glass rounds
4 antique faux malachite
    8mm art glass rounds
2 vintage tortoise-shell
    10mm art glass rounds
1½" Karmul finish filigree connector*
½" filigree clasp*
3 Karmul finish ¾" filigree connectors*

15 Karmul finish 7mm bead caps*
40 Karmul finish 4mm jump rings*
5 Karmul finish 1" headpins*
24 Karmul finish 1" eyepins*
6" length 3mm Karmul finish chain*
*Available through Karmul Studios

Toolbox

Wire cutters
Round nose pliers
Flat nose pliers

Here's How to Assemble Beaded Portions with Filigree Embellishments:

1. Lay out the items you will need: beads, bead caps, eyepins, jump rings and filigree connectors.

2. Assemble bead components using eyepins, beads, and bead caps. Connect to filigree embellishment with jump rings.

3. This makes the beginning of off-shoots of this design.

Here's How to Assemble this Style of Vintage Jewelry:

1. Cut the chain (if applicable) to the desired lengths.

2. Arrange beads in order of desired jewelry design.

3. Slide the non-looped end of the eyepin through the center of the bead opening. If using bead caps, slide the non-looped end of the eyepin through the bead cap with cupped end facing the bead.

4. Hold the looped end of the eyepin firmly to the bead and using a pair of round-nose jewelry pliers, make a loop with the non-looped end of the eyepin, making it as tight as possible. A secure bead is essential to the symmetry and quality of your jewelry.

5. Repeat steps 2 through 4 until all beads are looped on their eyepins.

6. Attach the completed beads to each other, to the pendant loop(s), or to the chain with jump rings using pliers.

7. Open the jump ring at the split by holding one side of the jump ring with one set of pliers and the other side with the other set of pliers, as detailed in Jump Ring Closures, page 34. Separate at the opening enough to slip the jump ring into the bead end loop, pendant loop or chain. Before closing, slip the same jump ring into the next bead end, pendant loop or chain. Close using the same technique as opening.

8. Attach the clasp to the remaining bead end loops or chain with the jump rings, using the same technique as in step 7.

Heirloom Necklace and Earrings

Designer: *Wendy Mullane*

Necklace
Finished Size: 17" without clasp
Where to Get It: From the artist
Time to Complete: One week
How Much Will It Cost? A manicure ($20 to $50)

Earrings
Finished Size: 1¾" without ear wires
Where to Get It: From the artist
Time to Complete: One hour
How Much Will It Cost? A movie and popcorn (less than $20)

Tips

● Refer to the instructions on page 107 for how to assemble this type of vintage jewelry.

● Bead catalogs offer products that add a protective coating to the tips of your pliers. Simply dip your pliers into this rubberized material following manufacturer's directions. The coating will prevent your pliers from scratching the filigrees finish.

Always a classic, black-and-gold is beautifully executed in amber, tortoise-shell matte art glass and antique jet glass in this timeless ensemble.

What You Need

Necklace
30mm vintage Czech faceted glass stone
6 tortoise-shell 14mm matte art glass rounds
2 deep amber 15mm glass rounds
2 black-and-gold 13mm foil art glass rounds
2 antique jet-black 12mm faceted glass rounds
2 antique jet-black 3mm glass rounds
4 antique jet-black 5mm glass rounds
2 vintage amber 16mm faceted glass teardrops

½" filigree clasp*
2" Karmul finish filigree wrap*
⅝" Karmul finish filigree connector*
2 Karmul finish 6mm bead caps*
2 Karmul finish 15mm x 5 mm filigree oval beads*
22-gauge brass wire

Earrings
2 vintage jet-black 18mm molded glass stones
2 vintage amber 16mm faceted glass teardrops

2 Karmul finish ⅝" filigree wraps*
2 Karmul finish 8mm bead caps*
2 Karmul finish 1" headpins*
2 Karmul finish 4mm jump rings*
2 kidney-shaped ear wires*
*Available through Karmul Studios

Toolbox
Wire cutters
Round nose pliers
Flat nose pliers

Here's How to Embellish the Stone:

1. Once you choose your center stone, choose your filigree. The filigree must be large enough to wrap around and secure the stone.

2. Bend the edges of the filigree in the exact shape of the stone, using your pliers (choose which ones give you the best hold on the filigree).

3. Set your stone inside the filigree (you may have to lift a couple of the edges to fit it in).

4. Once the stone is inside the filigree, secure it by symmetrically tightening down the edges against the stone. This will take some practice. Be sure to have plenty of filigrees on hand while in the learning stages.

5. Leave adequate room to insert a jump ring for hanging.

Tip

● The filigree will not scratch the stone; however, take care to avoid marring the stone with the pliers.

Here's How to Connect the Pendant to the Filigree Embellishment:

1. Secure the bead and bead caps on the eyepin.

2. Connect the beaded sections to the filigree embellishment. This serves as a connector centerpiece with the jump rings.

3. Connect the bead section and filigree embellishment to the pendant.

ear wire

filigree wrap

jet-black stone

bead cap

faceted glass teardrop

filigree clasp

bead cap

filigree oval bead

bead cap

jet-black faceted round

amber faceted teardrop

black-and-gold foil glass round

jet-black glass round

deep amber round

jet-black glass round

tortoise-shell round

filigree wrap

faceted glass stone

filigree connector

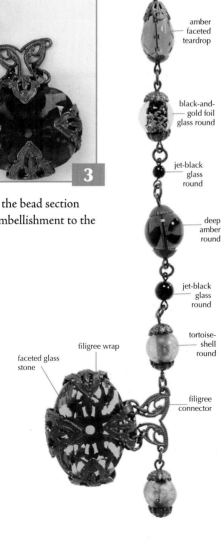

Opera House Cuff Bracelet

Designer: *Wendy Mullane*

Finished Size: Adjustable, 6" to 7" without clasp
Where to Get It: From the artist
Time to Complete: One weekend
How Much Will It Cost? A movie and popcorn
(less than $20)

What You Need to Know

Note: The stone used in these how-to photographs
differs from the project shot, as it is a thumbstone
semiprecious agate, not a vintage Czech faceted glass
oval stone. The agate is available in rock shops.

What You Need

25mm vintage Czech faceted glass oval stone
9 vintage sapphire 3mm faceted glass ovals
Karmul finish filigree wrap*
2 Karmul finish filigree connectors*
1" Karmul finish headpin*
8 Karmul finish 1" eyepins*
26 Karmul finish 4mm jump rings*
Karmul finish lobster clasp*
3" Karmul finish chain*
*Available through Karmul Studios

Toolbox

Wire cutters
Round pliers
Flat nose pliers

*As deep as the sea and as wide as the sky, the sapphire blue of the
vintage Czech faceted glass stone and beads in this bracelet will whisk
you away to your own private dream.*

Here's How to Wrap a Contemporary Stone with a Filigree Bead Setting:

1. Lay out the various components needed.

2. Open the filigree wrap.

3. Turn the ends of the filigree in with your needle nose pliers.
Set stone inside loose setting.

4. Bend the filigree down around the stone to secure the stone in
the setting. Attach jump rings in top for pendant hanger.

Tip

● Refer to the instructions on page 107 for how to assemble this type of
vintage jewelry.

Watercolor Choker

The way the light dances on the colorful vintage foiled glass stones in this stunning choker will capture attention as well as the imagination.

Designer: *Wendy Mullane*

Finished Size: 13¾" without clasp
Where to Get It: From the artist
Time to Complete: One week
How Much Will It Cost? A manicure ($20 to $50)

What You Need
4 vintage Czech harlequin art glass 20mm stones
Vintage Czech harlequin art glass 25mm stone
6 vintage Czech harlequin art glass
   marquise 12mm stones
2 vintage fuchsia 5mm foil art glass rounds
2 opalescent mottled 5mm flashed glass rounds
2 green-and-gold 10mm art glass ovals
2 vintage iridescent 13mm art glass rectangles
2 vintage pink-and-green 11mm art glass twisted beads
6 Karmul finish ⅝" filigree wraps*
5 Karmul finish 1½" filigree wraps*
4 Karmul finish 8mm bead caps*
½" Karmul finish filigree clasp*
10 Karmul finish 1" eyepins*
22 Karmul finish 4mm jump rings*
*Available through Karmul Studios

Toolbox
Wire cutters
Round nose pliers
Flat nose pliers

filigree clasp
art glass twisted bead
mottled flashed glass round
green-and-gold art glass oval
art glass rectangle
fuchsia foil glass round
marquis art glass stone
art glass stones
filigree wrap
art glass stone

Here's How to Encase the Vintage Stone:

1. Once you choose your center stone, choose your filigree. The filigree must be large enough to wrap around and secure the stone. Open the filigree bead at end sections.

2. Begin creating the setting by turning the ends of the bead in with your needle nose pliers. Set stone inside the loose setting.

3. Crimp down the bead around the stone in the setting. Once secure, attach jump rings to the top openings for the pendant hanger.

Here's How to Attach the Filigree Encased Glass Adornments to One Another:

1. Separate adornments.

2. Attach two adornments to each other.

3. Attach third filigree encased glass adornment to the other side of the center pendant.

filigree clasp

pink art glass oval

cranberry art glass round

pearl

glass baroque

art glass twisted bead

fuchsia art glass round

bead cap

bead cap

Signature Artistic Ensemble Set

Designer: *Wendy Mullane*

Necklace
Finished Size: 14" top strand/ 25" bottom strand without clasp
Where to Get It: From the artist
Time to Complete: One week
How Much Will It Cost?
One-way ticket to London (more than $100)

Bracelet
Finished Size: 7¾" without clasp
Where to Get It: From the artist
Time to Complete: One weekend
How Much Will It Cost?
A movie and popcorn (less than $20)

Earrings
Finished Size:
1½" without ear wires
Where to Get It: From the artist
Time to Complete: One weekend
How Much Will It Cost?
A movie and popcorn (less than $20)

Tip
● Refer to the instructions on page 107 for how to assemble this type of vintage jewelry.

ear wire

cranberry satin glass tube

olive glass bicone

filigree wrap

fuchsia glass scarab cabochon

This amazing necklace has the ability of a chameleon to transform. The bracelet could be worn separately, but when the need arises, the bracelet clasp can be fastened into the necklace clasp to give the piece a whole new length and dimension. What a clever way to extend your jewelry wardrobe.

What You Need

Necklace
30mm vintage bird-of-paradise Czech glass stone
2 cranberry 4mm art glass rounds
4 vintage Cloisonné 8mm rounds
2 plum 5mm art glass rounds
2 plum 12mm art glass rounds
2 moss green 5mm art glass rounds
2 moss green 10mm art glass rounds
2 fuchsia 10mm vintage West German art glass rounds
2 genuine sea 6mm pearls
2 vintage fuchsia 5mm foil art glass rounds
2 vintage pink satin 4mm rounds
2 vintage light pink 5mm art glass ovals
4 vintage light pink 8mm art glass ovals
4 fuchsia 7mm miracle bead ovals
2 vintage pink-and-brown 9mm mottled art glass ovals
3 olivine 13mm mottled foiled art glass ovals
4 olive 3mm glass bicones
4 vintage opalescent 10mm glass baroques

2 vintage West German striped olivine 13mm baroques
2 vintage pink-and-green 11mm art glass twisted beads
½" filigree clasp*
2¼" Karmul finish filigree wrap*
8mm x 5mm Karmul finish barrel
49 Karmul finish 2" eyepins*
56 Karmul finish 4mm jump rings*
42 Karmul finish 8mm bead caps*
½" Karmul finish filigree wrap*
2 Karmul finish ¾" filigree connectors*
2" Karmul finish 4mm chain*
22-gauge Karmul finish wire

Bracelet
2 cranberry 4mm art glass rounds
2 genuine sea 6mm pearls
2 opalescent 10mm glass baroques
2 vintage pink-and-green 11mm art glass twisted beads
2 vintage light pink 5mm art glass ovals
10mm fuchsia vintage West German art glass round

6 Karmul finish 8mm bead caps*
4 Karmul finish 5mm bead caps*
12 Karmul finish 4mm jump rings*
11 Karmul finish 2" eyepins*
1" Karmul finish filigree clasp*

Earrings
2 vintage fuchsia glass scarab 10mm cabochons
2 olive 3mm glass bicones
2 cranberry 4mm satin glass tubes
2 Karmul finish 1" filigree wraps*
4 Karmul finish 1" eyepins*
4 Karmul finish 4mm jump rings*
2 Karmul finish kidney-shaped ear wires*

*Available through Karmul Studios

Toolbox
Wire cutters
Round nose pliers
Flat nose pliers

Here's How to Attach the Necklace and Filigree Embellishments to the Clasp:

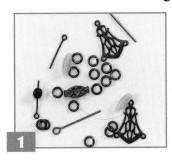

1. Individual unattached parts.

2. Open jump ring on clasp.

3. Slide jump ring through embellishment and close to secure. See finished side of clasp.

filigree clasp

filigree connector

pink art glass oval

bead cap

cloisonné round

olive glass bicone

art glass twisted bead

plum art glass round

olivine mottled foiled art glass oval

pink satin round

pearl

glass baroque

moss green art glass round

pink-and-brown mottled art glass oval

olivine striped baroque

plum art glass round

fuchsia art glass round

pink art glass oval

glass stone

- aqua glass round
- bead cap
- aqua teardrop
- green twisted bead
- amber disc
- seafoam green rectangle
- brown art glass round
- foiled art glass round
- pearl
- miracle bead
- faux malachite round

- faceted glass stone
- marine dolphin embellishment

Of the Sea Necklace

Designer: *Jeanne Holland*

Finished Size: 20" without clasp
Where to Get It: From the artist
Time to Complete: One week
How Much Will It Cost?
A manicure ($20 to $50)

What You Need

30mm vintage Czech faceted glass stone
1" x 1¾" ancient marine dolphin embellishment*
4 aqua glass 3mm rounds
2 light blue miracle beads 3mm rounds
2 antique faux malachite art glass 8mm rounds
2 genuine olivine 6mm round sea pearls
2 aquamarine 12mm foiled art glass rounds
2 mossy brown 5mm art glass rounds
2 teal 5mm art glass rounds
2 aqua glass 10mm teardrops
2 amber glass 9mm disks
2 antique pearlized seafoam green 15mm rectangles
2 vintage iridescent green art glass 11mm twisted beads
½" filigree clasp*
2" Karmul finish filigree wrap*
45mm x 30mm Karmul finish fish finding*
24 Karmul finish 1" eyepins*
36 Karmul finish 4mm jump rings*
22 Karmul finish 7mm bead caps*
3" Karmul finish 3mm chain*

*Available through Karmul Studios

Toolbox

Wire cutters
Round nose pliers
Flat nose pliers

Light washes over the aqua waves of glass behind a sea serpent finding. The shades of mossy green to aquamarine in vintage art glass and sea pearls completes the illusion.

What You Need to Know

1. Lay out the components you need: beads, eyepins, bead caps and jump rings.

2. Place a bead cap, bead and another bead cap on the eyepin.

3. Turn a loop on the other end to secure.

4. Repeat for each eyepin, varying some to not include bead caps.

5. Use jump rings to connect the components.

Tapestry Evening Choker

filigree clasp

teal art glass round

filigree connector

jump ring

looped eye pin

filigree wrap

faceted glass stone

Designer: *Wendy Mullane*

Finished Size: 12½" without clasp
Where to Get It: From the artist
Time to Complete: One week
How Much Will It Cost? A manicure ($20 to $50)

What You Need

25mm vintage Czech
  faceted glass stone
12 teal 5mm art glass rounds
12 Karmul finish 1" eyepins*
34 Karmul finish
  4mm jump rings*
2 Karmul finish
  7mm jump rings*
½" Karmul finish filigree clasp*
6 Karmul finish
  1⅛" filigree connectors*
2" Karmul finish filigree wrap*

*Available through Karmul Studios

Toolbox

Wire cutters
Round nose pliers
Flat nose pliers

The deep teal of the Czech glass sparkles against the patina of the filigree metal findings to create this lacework that is just waiting to encircle a delicate neck.

Tip

●Refer to the instructions on page 107 for how to assemble this type of vintage jewelry.

Here's How to Assemble Choker Filigree Embellishment:

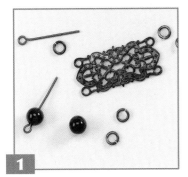

1

5

1. Lay out the components you will need: beads, eyepins, connectors and jump rings.

2. Open jump rings.

3. Thread beads on eyepins.

4. Turn loop on end of eyepin.

5. Use jump rings to attach eyepin components to filigree and close to secure.

Caterpillar Bracelet

Designer: *Susan Ray*

Finished Size: 7½" without clasp
Where to Get It: Craft stores
Time to Complete: One weekend
How Much Will It Cost? A movie and popcorn (less than $20)

What You Need to Know

See the instructions and information outlined in Single-Strand Basics, pages 23-27, plus the specific steps detailed below.

Here's How:

1. Clamp a hemostat tightly to the very end of the three wires and string on one teardrop to each wire.

2. String each wire through one hole of the first space bar, as shown.

3. Continue to string on more teardrops alternating colors, adding another spacer for each 1" of length.

4. Complete strands by stringing one additional teardrop to each wire.

5. Test for proper fit before adding clasp.

6. Add crimp bead to one finished wire, string through one loop on clasp, and then back through crimp bead.

7. Test for proper fit again and then crimp the bead and clip the excess wire tail.

8. Repeat steps 6 and 7 for the remaining two strands.

9. Repeat steps 6 through 8 for the other clasp end.

What You Need
58 clear aurora borealis
  6mm x 8mm briolettes*
58 amethyst transparent
  6mm x 8mm briolettes*
58 light blue transparent
  6mm x 8mm briolettes*
8 silver three-hole spacer bars
Sterling silver three-strand clasp
6 sterling silver 2mm x 3mm
  crimp beads
3 pieces of 12" flexible wire
*Available through Halcraft

Toolbox
Wire cutters
Flat nose pliers

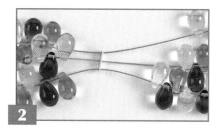

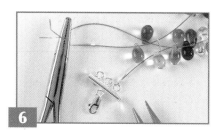

This caterpillar truly dances around the wrist. The glistening briolettes are cleverly contained by concealed spacer bars.

Sue's Blues Necklace

Finding a unique way to show this lampwork bead developed into a fun stringing project. To make it into a pendant, it is set off by coral chips and royal blue beads.

Here's How:

The focal bead was made into a pendant by stringing the design from the center.

1. Cut your wire to a 27" length.

2. Thread on a coral nugget and slide it to the center of the wire.

3. String on four 11/0 seed beads, one 6/0 bead and four 11/0 seed beads on each side of nugget.

4. Take the ends of both wires and thread together through one disc, the lampwork focal bead and one disc.

5. Separate the wires.

6. Thread 10 11/0 seed beads on each wire.

7. Take first wire end and thread through the green rectangle bead from right to left.

8. Thread the second wire end through the same bead from left to right. This will position your wire to go in opposite directions.

9. Thread a seed bead on each wire end for space before continuing to string the pattern.

10. Finish as in Single-Strand Basics, pages 23-27.

Designer: *Sue Wilke*

Necklace

Finished Size: 23" without clasp
Where to Get It: Specialty bead shops or catalogs; craft stores
Time to Complete: One weekend
How Much Will It Cost? A manicure ($20 to $50)

What You Need to Know

See the instructions and information outlined in Single-Strand Basics, pages 23-27 as well as the pendant instructions below.

What You Need

22mm x 22mm blue-and-green lampwork bead
7 coral chips
38 lapis 3mm x 6mm to 4mm x 10mm chips
12mm x 6mm green glass barrel
10 royal blue 6/0 seed beads
8 dark blue 2mm x 8mm discs
20 dark green 3mm x 4mm barrels
2 red-and-clear 3mm x 4mm barrels
124 red opaque 11/0 seed beads
84 dark blue opaque 11/0 seed beads
2 sterling silver 2mm x 3mm crimp beads
Sterling silver S-hook clasp
27" flexible wire

Toolbox

Wire cutters
Flat nose or chain nose pliers
Round nose pliers

---

royal blue seed bead

dark blue opaque seed bead

red opaque seed bead

green glass barrel

red-and-clear glass barrel

coral chip

lapis chip

lampwork focal bead

dark blue disc

She Sells Seashells Amulet Bag

Designer: *Claire Russ*

Finished Size: 15½" length
Where to Get It: Specialty bead shops or catalogs; craft stores
Time to Complete: One week
How Much Will It Cost? A manicure ($20 to $50)

What You Need to Know

See the instructions and information outlined in Single-Strand Basics, pages 23-27.

What You Need

550 green 11/0 seed beads
2,960 pearl gray 11/0 seed beads
140 silver-lined clear 11/0 seed beads
4 teal transparent 4mm rounds
4 green transparent 4mm rounds
4 yellow/green transparent 4mm rounds
7 light blue transparent 4mm rounds
2 blue opaque 4mm rounds
3 aqua opaque 4mm rounds
6 yellow/green matte 4mm rounds
2 light green matte 8mm rounds
10mm x 6mm aqua wire-wrapped tube
2 aqua matte 10mm x 6mm tube
3 clear aurora borealis matte 14mm x 14mm shell beads
14mm x 5mm olivine wire-wrapped tube
3 aqua transparent 14mm x 6mm fish beads
18mm x 18mm teal matte fish bead
18mm x 18mm green clear fish bead
Silamide A or Nymo D thread*
Big-eye beading needle
*Available through specialty bead shops and catalogs

Toolbox

Wire cutters
Flat nose or chain nose pliers

Treasures collected while strolling the beach are immortalized in the waves of this amulet bag. Even the sheer droplets of water are captured in time in its net pattern.

Here's How to Make the Bag Body:

1. String on a stopper bead, followed by 37 pearl gray seed beads and two aqua beads.

2. Turn around: Go back through the second aqua bead from your needle, in the opposite direction, so that now you will be working towards your starting point. String on five gray beads and then go through the sixth gray bead on the initial strand, as shown.

3. String on five more pearl gray beads, then go through the sixth gray bead down again. You will be forming little diamonds, working towards your stopper bead. When you reach your stopper bead, you will have a chain of six little diamonds.

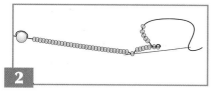

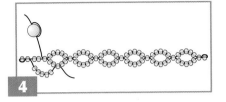

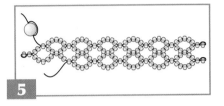

Tip

• It helps to think of your stopper bead as the bottom of the work and your first turnaround point as the top. You'll work up, then turn around and work back down again and then back up. To try to aim for the illusion of drops of water in the net, replace a gray bead with an aqua bead.

1. String on a starter bead, then string on one silver bead, seven gray beads, one silver and one focal bead. In this case, alternate ocean character beads and 4mm spheres. Repeat until you have a long enough string of beads to easily go over your head.

2. Go through the top turnaround bead on one edge of the top of your bag, run your needle through the adjoining beads, out through the next point, and then start back up for the second strand.

3. Begin by repeating the pattern of the first strand: one silver, seven grays, one silver, and the character or sphere beads. Repeat until you have a chain of two strands of beads, held together by a larger bead every ½" or so.

4. When you get back to the other end of your neck chain, secure at the opposite side point of the bag. At this point you have your neck chain attached at one point on one side of the bag, two on the other.

4. Add two gray beads, two aqua beads and turn around. String on five pearl gray beads and go through the middle bead of the first diamond, as shown.

5. String on five more pearl gray beads and go through the middle bead of the second diamond. Continue in this manner until you reach the other end of the chain of beads. You now have a wider chain and can see the pattern clearly at the end of the row: two gray beads, two aqua beads and turn around.

6. Continue adding rows of the stitch until you have a rectangle of netting about 4" wide, work your way until you are on the opposite end of the work as your stopper bead.

Here's How to Add the Neck Strap:

5. Look at the bag, run your needle through the appropriate beads to get to a second point, remove the stopper bead and knot off.

6. The third strand going through the neck chain is a long, single strand of mostly aqua beads with random silver beads added. This is tied off at a third point adjacent to the gray chain, then runs through all the loops, and tied off at a third point on the opposite side.

7. At this point, you can run your needle through your beadwork and stitch various ocean themed beads

7. Turn around, string two gray beads on, go through the middle bead of the first diamond *on the opposite side of the work*. You will connect the last row of stringing to the first row.

8. Now "zip up" the rectangle into a tube by stringing on two gray beads, then going through the center bead of the opposing end of the work, then back-and-forth until you hit the end. You now have a tube.

Here's How to Add the Bottom:

1. Starting at one point in the bag body, add two aqua beads, continue thread through the opposite point, add two more aqua beads and go back again, to give a wavy effect.

onto your netted bag body for embellishments, as shown.

8. General for all beadwork: You are now done, but all beaders should bear in mind that the beads are glass held together by thread, and glass cuts thread. As tedious as it sometimes seems, it is a good idea to needle through as many areas as possible to reinforce the stitching. Some beaders use a double-thread to begin with, but since so many beads have to be passed through multiple times, you can run into trouble by filling the beads with too much thread and not being able to get your needle through when you need it to.

Tip

• This project and the Wine Country Amulet Bag that follows use size 11 seed beads, but there are still a wide variety of differences between brands and country of manufacture. Czech seed beads tend to be a bit more irregular, while Japanese Dynamites are more regular and Japanese delicas are the top of the line. The latter are considerably more expensive, but give such an even result that you might think a finished project was made by computer. They tend to be preferred by artists who really paint a picture with peyote stitch. Delicas are also smaller than most other size 11 beads, which is a consideration in overall finished size of the project.

Wine Country Amulet Bag

Designer: *Claire Russ*

Finished Size: 15" length
Where to Get It: Specialty bead shops or catalogs; craft stores
Time to Complete: One week
How Much Will It Cost? A manicure ($20 to $50)

What You Need
1,525 amber transparent
  11/0 seed beads
960 amber matte 11/0 seed beads
139 gold transparent
  11/0 seed beads
16 green transparent
  11/0 seed beads
4 light purple aurora borealis
  6mm rounds
7 tanzanite purple 4mm rounds
6 magenta transparent 4mm rounds
3 dark magenta 4mm rounds
5 lavender matte 4mm rounds
3 black-and-dark pink 4mm rounds
4 light purple aurora borealis
  4mm rounds
3 lavender transparent 4mm rounds
3 black-and-dark purple
  4mm rounds
4 blue-and-purple transparent
  4mm rounds
4 green aurora borealis matte
  16mm x 14mm leaf beads
2 green transparent
  20mm x 12mm grape beads
25mm x 15mm purple
  transparent grape bead
2 gold wire coils
Forest green wire coil
Silamide A or Nymo D thread*
Big-eye beading needle
*Available through specialty bead shops and catalogs

Toolbox
Wire cutters
Flat nose or chain nose pliers

Grapes, vines and leaves reminiscent of a day in wine country show off against the basket weave look of the checkered pattern of matte and shiny seed beads.

What You Need to Know

This bag is geared to someone who is not new to beading, but may be trying peyote stitch for the first time. Tubular peyote stitch (even-count in this case) can be easier than flat peyote in that you don't have to worry about as many ragged edges and you can choose which side is the front of the bag after you're done with the purse part, which allows you to hide an error or two.

1. Single-thread your needle with 2 or 3 yards of Silamide A or Nymo D and add on a stopper bead.

2. String on 70 11/0 beads, which is 10 sets of seven beads in the following pattern—seven clear finish, seven matte, seven clear and so on.

3. Once the initial 70 beads are strung pass your needle back through the first four seed beads on the strand to form a circle.

4. Add a seed bead, skip over the fifth bead on the strand, and pass through the sixth. Continue adding a bead, skipping the next bead in the round, and then passing through every other. To establish the pattern, you will be adding clear beads over the clear beads and matte over matte. In this round, that will be four clear, three matte, four clear, etc. This becomes rounds 1 and 2. The next round will be three clear, four matte and so on to continue the pattern.

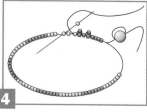

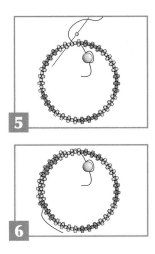

5. After you complete the second circle (round 2), pass through the fourth and fifth beads on the initial strand, as shown.

6. Continue to add on beads, skipping a bead between and entering the next bead over to complete round 3. You will find that the beads you skip will be "down beads" on the round and those you enter are "up beads."

7. Repeat step 6 until you have a 4" tube, or approximately 52 total rounds.

8. Remove the starter bead.

Here's How to Add the Bottom:

1. Be sure the "up beads" and "down beads" of the two bottom edges of the bag body fit together and interlock before you attempt to "zip" them together. If they don't line up, add one more round of beads and check again.

2. Starting at the endmost "up bead" at the bottom of the bag body, pass through an "up bead" from each side of the bottom, just as though you were closing a zipper.

Here's How to Make the Neck Straps and Embellishments:

1. Place a new length of thread on the needle and secure it on one corner of the top edge of the bag body.

2. String on a gold transparent 11/0 seed bead, seven amber transparent 11/0 seed beads, another gold transparent seed bead and then one of the 4mm rounds.

3. Repeat the step 2 pattern 33 more times and end the strand with a gold transparent seed bead, seven amber transparent seeds, a gold transparent seed bead, followed by a light purple 6mm round and a gold transparent seed bead.

4. Attach the strand to the other top edge of the bag body by needling through the top edge across to the corner you started on.

5. Go through the first gold transparent seed bead on the initial neck strap strand, add on seven amber transparent seed beads and a gold transparent seed bead.

6. Continue through the 4mm bead on the initial neck strap strand.

7. Repeat steps 5 and 6 until you've gone around the entire neck strap. When you reach the last gold transparent bead on the initial strand, pass through it again and add on a leaf bead, a gold transparent seed bead and two amber transparent seed beads.

8. Enter the bag body far enough down so that the leaf bead rests flat against the body.

9. Needle through a few beads horizontally and come back out so that you can add on two amber transparent seed beads and they travel back up through the existing gold transparent bead, leaf bead, gold transparent bead and needle through the stitching and tie off the string and hide the knot in the bag body stitching.

10. Add on another leaf bead to the other side of the bag.

11. Add in wire coils, as you like.

Here's How to Add Fringe:

1. Thread a new length of thread on the needle and pass through a dozen or so beads in bottom of the bag, coming out where you want your first strand of fringe to be.

2. String the beads you like on to your thread. In this case, the two fringes at the ends of the bottom of the Wine Country bag consist of the following pattern: one gold seed bead, one green seed bead, one gold seed bead, one 4mm purple, one gold seed bead, one green seed bead, one gold seed bead, five amber transparent seed beads, one gold seed bead, one green seed bead, one gold seed bead and seven amber seed beads. The grape bead is slid on and the needle is passed back up through from the bottom gold seed bead back to the top gold. Fringe tends to flow best if you have the larger beads at the bottom of your fringe.

3. Tie a knot to secure each fringe strand.

4. Run your thread through the amulet bag, coming out where you want the next strand of fringe to be.

5. The pattern of the second and fourth fringe strands on the Wine Country bag are: one gold seed bead, four amber transparent, one gold seed bead, one green seed bead, one gold seed bead, one 6mm purple, one gold seed bead, one green seed bead, one gold seed bead, seven amber

transparent seed beads, one gold seed bead, one green seed bead, one gold seed bead, a leaf bead and a gold seed bead. Make the turn and travel back up through from the bottom leaf to the top gold seed bead.

6. The pattern for the center and longest fringe strand is: one gold seed bead, seven amber transparent seed beads, one gold seed bead, one green seed bead, one gold seed bead, one 6mm purple round, one gold seed bead, one green seed bead, one gold seed bead, 15 amber transparent seed beads, one gold seed bead and seven amber transparent beads. Slide on the purple grape bead and turn around, entering back through the bottom gold seed bead and back up the fringe strand to the top gold seed bead.

Watches

Designer: *Alyson Leahy*

The Pink Sophia Watch
Finished Size: 6"
Where to Get It: Specialty bead shops or catalogs; craft stores
Time to Complete: One weekend
How Much Will It Cost? A manicure ($20 to $50)

The Green Isabelle Watch
Finished Size: 6¼"
Where to Get It: Specialty bead shops or catalogs; craft stores
Time to Complete: One weekend
How Much Will It Cost? A manicure ($20 to $50)

What You Need to Know
1. Lay out your pattern of beads and your watch face on a bead board. Note that next to the watch on each side you will need two each of five beads so the pattern will match.
2. Begin stringing by sliding wire through the watch face and centering the watch face on the wire.
3. Thread on your first five beads on each side of the watch face. They should be arranged symmetrically from the watch going out.
4. Take the ends of both wires and string them together through the rest of the beads on that side of the watchband
5. String on one crimp bead and thread wire end through the toggle, and back through the crimp bead and next three beads.
6. Take the other wire and thread it the opposite way through the toggle, back through the crimp bead and three beads.
7. Pull the wires taut.
8. Measure for a proper fit and then flatten the crimp and trim the wires.
9. Repeat steps 2 through 8 for other side of watchband.

You will feel like the belle of the ball with these bejeweled watches gracing your wrist.

What You Need

The Pink Sophia Watch
- 1 x 1¾" two-loop watch face
- 2 sterling silver 3mm x 3mm crimp beads
- 6 raspberry matte 6/0 seed beads
- 2 cranberry 6/0 seed beads
- 2 silver daisy 5mm x 2mm spacers
- 4 silver 6mm x 2mm spacer discs
- 4 silver 3mm rounds
- 6 pink synthetic 6mm cat's-eye rounds
- 2 pink swirl 12mm rounds
- 4 cranberry pink confetti 8mm rounds
- 4 silver 4mm x 3mm ribbed discs
- Silver heart toggle set
- 2 pieces of 12" flexible wire

The Green Isabelle Watch
- 1 x 1¾" two-loop silver watch face
- 6 silver 6mm x 2mm discs
- 2 silver 8mm x 2mm dimpled with ball ovals
- 2 silver rosebud 4mmx 2mm ovals
- 2 celadon green 8mm crackled rounds
- 6 dark green 8mm confetti rounds
- 8 silver 3mm ribbed rounds
- 2 celadon synthetic 6mm cats eyes
- 4 celadon synthetic 4mm cats eyes
- 2 turquoise green 16mm x 14mm nuggets
- 2 sterling silver 3mm x 3mm crimp beads
- Silver heart toggle set
- 2 pieces 12"-long flexible wire

Toolbox
Wire cutters   Flat nose or chain nose pliers

Chatelaine Cutter Necklace with Scissors Minder

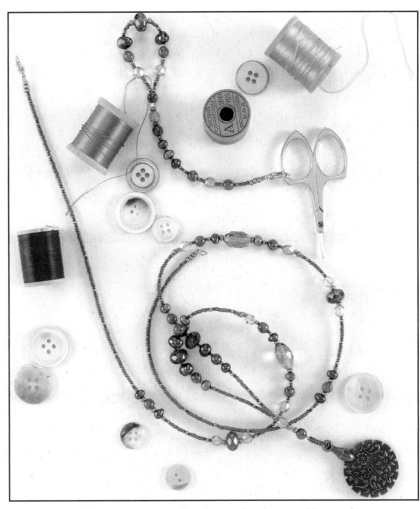

Reminiscent of the Victorian era, this elegant chatelaine necklace and scissors minder set could make any needleworker feel like a queen.

Designer: *Sue Wilke*

Chatelaine Cutter
Finished Size: 39" without clasp
Where to Get It: Specialty bead shops or catalogs; craft stores
Time to Complete: One afternoon
How Much Will It Cost? A manicure
($20 to $50)

Scissors Minder
Finished Size: 7½" without clasp
Where to Get It: Specialty bead shops or catalogs; craft stores
Time to Complete: One weekend
How Much Will It Cost? A movie and popcorn (less than $20)

What You Need to Know
See the instructions and information outlined in Single-Strand Basics, pages 23-29.

What You Need

Chatelaine Cutter
24 gold matte 8/0 seed beads
119 orange black-lined 11/0 seed beads
260 green matte 11/0 seed beads
54 gold matte 11/0 seed beads
13 teal-lined clear 8/0 seed beads
12 green freshwater pearl
   4mm x 6mm potato-shapes
11 turquoise 6mm glass rounds
9 peridot Czech fire 6mm faceted rounds
4 vintage 7mm x 10mm
   faceted crystal rondelle discs
2 vintage green-and-pink
   15mm x 9mm faceted barrels
4 green freshwater pearl
   7mm x 8mm potato-shapes

45mm x 30mm antiqued gold
   pendant cutter*
3 gold 2mm x 3mm crimp beads
Gold lobster clasp
6mm gold jump ring
43" flexible wire
*Cutters available in most craft and fabric stores

Scissors Minder
7 gold matte 8/0 seed beads
10 orange black-lined 11/0 seed beads
23 green matte 11/0 seed beads
15 gold matte 11/0 seed beads
2 teal-lined clear 8/0 seed beads
3 green freshwater pearl
   4mm x 6mm potato-shapes

2 green freshwater pearl
   7mm x 8mm potato-shapes
6 turquoise howlite 6mm rounds
4 peridot Czech fire 6mm faceted rounds
7mm x 10mm vintage faceted
   crystal rondelle disc
Gold thread/sewing scissors*
2mm x 3mm gold crimp bead
Gold lobster clasp set
12" flexible wire
*Sewing scissors available in most craft and fabric stores

Toolbox
Wire cutters
Flat nose or chain nose pliers

Grab Bag Party Bracelets

Designers: *Linda Duhme, Brenda Duhme, Jill Schwenker, Laureen Schwenker, Elizabeth Malone, Lotralee Malone, Kelly Laugesen, Julie Ann Duhme, Amber Malone and Linda Duhme Olson*

Finished Sizes: 7½" without clasp
Where to Get It: Specialty bead shops or catalogs; craft stores
Time to Complete: One evening or afternoon
How Much Will It Cost? A movie and popcorn (less than $20)

Loralee

Julie Ann

Amber

What You Need

Assortment of beads in various sizes and colors (quantities depends on number of bracelets needed)
Silver round toggle set (per bracelet)
12" flexible wire (per bracelet)

Toolbox

Wire cutters
Flat nose or chain nose pliers

What You Need to Know

See the instructions and information outlined in Single-Strand Basics, pages 23-29.

Tip

● Bracelets are so easy to make, they are a great beginner's project. If you have a friend who is a little hesitant to explore her own design skills, encourage her with the fact that with 20 beads in 20 minutes, she'll be proud to say she made it herself.

Tip

● Have a jewelry party yourself. It will delight your friends and give you an opportunity to share your skills. Some very fine bead stores offer walk-in classes; many now offer them on-demand. So take your family and friends along next time you visit your local beadery. Shop owners are always willing to share a tip or trick or two. It will become a treasured memory. Beading spans all generations. We have hosted many grandmothers who want to remake a necklace for a granddaughter; mothers and daughters who make matching sets; and friends who want to share a day together. These are great for birthday parties, bridal parties and reunions.

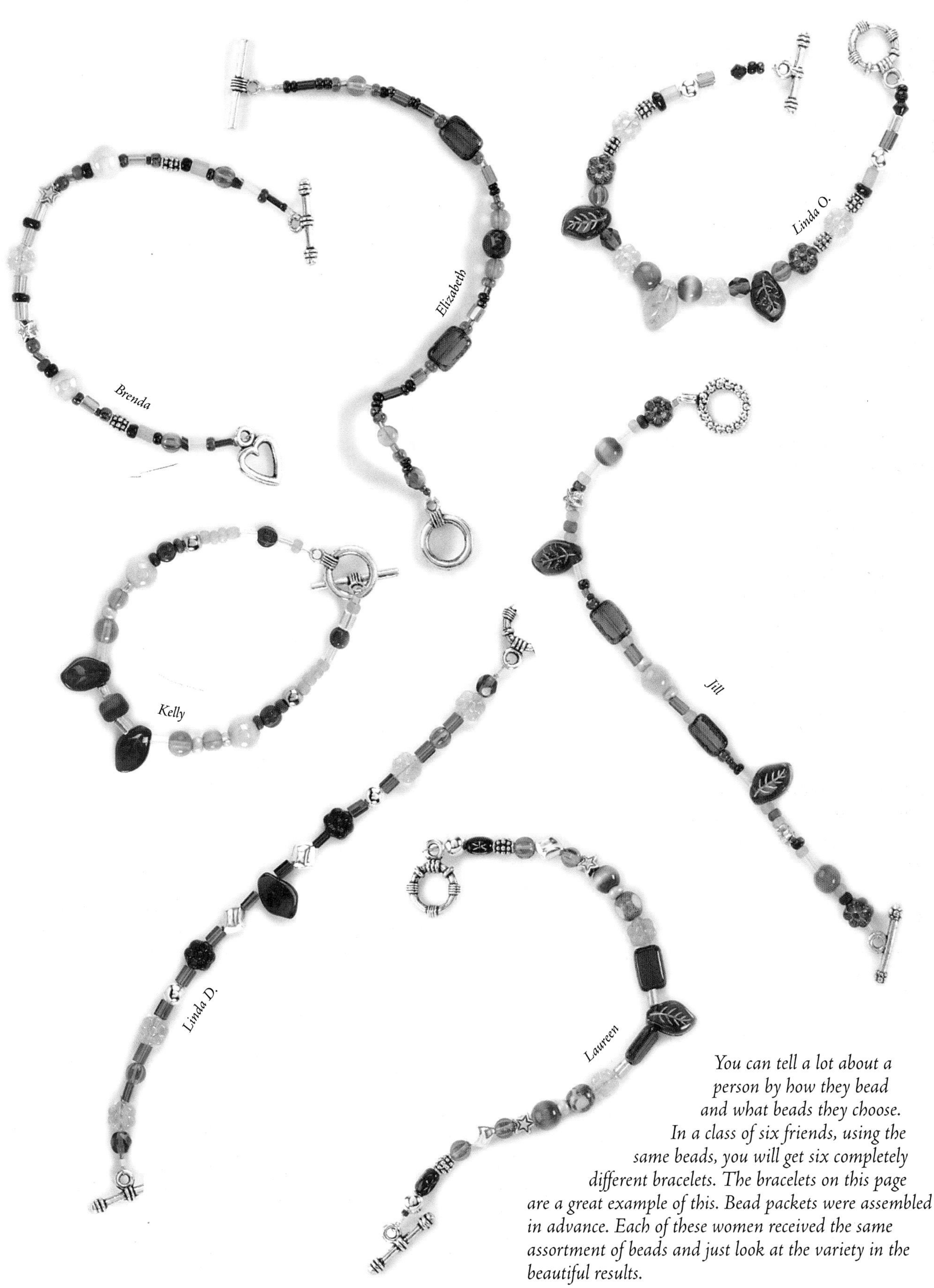

Elizabeth

Linda O.

Brenda

Jill

Kelly

Linda D.

Lauren

You can tell a lot about a
person by how they bead
and what beads they choose.
In a class of six friends, using the
same beads, you will get six completely
different bracelets. The bracelets on this page
are a great example of this. Bead packets were assembled
in advance. Each of these women received the same
assortment of beads and just look at the variety in the
beautiful results.

Sterling Cubes Personalized Bracelets

Designer: *Carol Coyle*

Cougar Mom Bracelet

Finished Size: 6¾" without clasp
Where to Get It: Specialty bead shops or catalogs; craft stores
Time to Complete: One weekend
How Much Will It Cost? A manicure ($20 to $50)

All-Star Bracelet

Finished Size: 6¾" without clasp
Where to Get It: Specialty bead shops or catalogs; craft stores
Time to Complete: One weekend
How Much Will It Cost? A manicure ($20 to $50)

Mom's Names Bracelet

Finished Size: 6¾" without clasp
Where to Get It: Specialty bead shops or catalogs; craft stores
Time to Complete: One weekend
How Much Will It Cost? A manicure ($20 to $50)

These timeless sterling silver and gold-filled creations are an "always to be cherished" commemoration. The crystals can sparkle as birthstones or school colors, while sterling cubes show off names. What a perfect gift for mom or grandma to celebrate the birth of a child, or for coach and player to display extraordinary team spirit. The possibilities are endless.

What You Need

Cougar Mom Bracelet
22 sterling silver 4mm rounds
12 gold-filled 4mm rounds
18 gold-filled 3mm rounds
8 blue 6mm faceted rounds
4 sterling silver 5mm x 6mm barrels
4.5mm alphabet blocks, as follows:
    1 "C", 2 "O", 1 "U", 1 "G", 1 "A",
    1 "R", 2 "M"
18 sterling silver 4mm daisy beads
2 two-hole 2mm spacers
11 gold-filled 4mm rounds
    (for between letters)
4 sterling silver 2mm x 3mm crimp beads
12" flexible wire (per strand)

All-Star Bracelet
4 red 6mm crystal bicones
4 blue 6mm crystal bicones
4 (6mm) crystal bicones
12 gold 4mm rounds
4 gold 5mm rounds
5.5mm alphabet blocks, as follows:
    2 "A", 2 "L", 2 "S", 1 "T", 1 "R"
11 gold 4.5mm daisy beads
Gold toggle set
2 gold 2mm x 3mm crimp beads
12" flexible wire

Toolbox
Wire cutters
Flat nose or chain nose pliers

Mom's Names Bracelet
4 6mm birthstones for each name
20 gold 4mm rounds
6 silver 3mm rounds
18 gold 5mm rounds
2 gold 5mm rounds
6 silver 4mm x 10mm barrels
4.5mm alphabet blocks,
    as necessary for each name
6 silver 4mm twists
6 gold 5mm twists
26 silver 5mm daisy beads
2 three-hole spacers
9 gold 4mm spacers for
    in between alpha beads
24 silver 5mm rondelles
Sterling silver three-strand toggle set
6 sterling silver 2mm x 3mm crimp beads
12" flexible wire (per strand)

Birthstones and Birth Gems

Aquarius (January): Garnet

Pisces (February): Amethyst

Aries (March): Aquamarine or bloodstone

Taurus (April): Diamonds, crystals, rhinestones or cubic zirconia

Gemini (May): Emeralds or agates

Cancer (June): Alexandrite or pearls

Leo (July): Ruby or onyx

Virgo (August): Peridot or carnelian

Libra (September): Sapphire or lapis

Scorpio (October): Pink tourmaline, rose quartz or opal

Sagittarius (November): Topaz or amber

Capricorn (December): Turquoise

What You Need to Know

See the instructions and information outlined in Single-Strand Basics, pages 23-29, as well as those in Multi-Strand Basics, pages 30-31.

Always string the names first and work from the middle out. (A set of hemostats holding the very ends of your wire while you string will make this task simple.) Spacers or rounds are strung next to the alphabet cubes to nestle inside for a better fit and look.

Tip

● You can change the colors of the faceted rounds and the mascot name to match your school colors and team. Really show your support for your children by adding charms representing the sports they play.

● If you have a friend who is ill, "remember me" bracelets will delight all who know her. Make a prayer bracelet for your ill friend and then one for each person who knows her. You can even add a heart or her initials if you like. Each time one wears the bracelet, your ill friend receives an extra thoughtful prayer.

Cougar Mom Bracelet

blue faceted round · sterling silver barrel · alphabet block · sterling silver daisy bead · toggle ring end

All-Star Bracelet

red crystal bicone · gold spacer · blue crystal bicone · alphabet block · clear crystal bicone · gold round

Mom's Names Bracelet

three-hole toggle clasp · birthstone beads · three-hole spacer · gold round · alphabet block · spacer · silver twist · sterling silver barrel

127

Bridal Jewelry Party

Designer: *Shannon Williams*

Sarah Dangle Bracelet with Silver Rhinestones
Finished Size: 7½" without clasp
Where to Get It: Craft stores
Time to Complete: One afternoon
How Much Will It Cost? A movie and popcorn (less than $20)

Jessica Dangle Bracelet with Pearl Seed Beads
Finished Size: 7" without clasp
Where to Get It: Craft stores
Time to Complete: One afternoon
How Much Will It Cost? A movie and popcorn (less than $20)

Kristen Bracelet with Silver Rhinestones
Finished Size: 7½" without clasp
Where to Get It: Craft stores
Time to Complete: One afternoon
How Much Will It Cost? A movie and popcorn (less than $20)

Using the same beads and pearls, but with unique patterns, these bracelets coordinate the bridesmaids, but still let their individuality shine through.

What You Need

Sarah Dangle Bracelet with Silver Rhinestones
- 21 white pearlized 4mm rounds
- 10 white pearlized 6mm rounds
- 2 silver aurora borealis Czech 6mm rounds
- 2 silver rhinestone 6mm rondelles
- 8mm silver rhinestone round
- 13 red transparent 11/0 seed beads
- 3 Siam 4mm faceted crystal bicones
- 2 clear 4mm x 6mm faceted crystal bicones
- 2 sterling silver 2mm x 3mm crimp beads
- 3" sterling silver headpin
- Silver round toggle set
- 12" flexible wire

Jessica Dangle Bracelet with Pearl Seed Beads
- 20 white pearlized 4mm rounds
- 10 white pearlized 6mm rounds
- 2 silver aurora borealis Czech 6mm rounds
- 2 silver rhinestone 6mm rondelles
- 8mm silver rhinestone round
- 16 red transparent 11/0 seed beads
- 3 Siam 4mm faceted crystal bicones
- 2 clear 4mm x 6mm faceted crystal bicones
- 2 sterling silver 2mm x 3mm crimp beads
- 3" sterling silver headpin
- Silver round toggle set
- 12" flexible wire

Kristen Bracelet with Silver Rhinestones
- 18 white pearlized 4mm rounds
- 8 white pearlized 6mm rounds
- 2 silver aurora borealis Czech 6mm rounds
- 4 silver rhinestone 6mm rondelles
- 8mm silver rhinestone round
- 24 red transparent 11/0 seed beads
- 2 Siam 4mm faceted crystal bicones
- 2 clear 4mm x 6mm faceted crystal bicones
- 2 sterling silver 2mm x 3mm crimp beads
- Silver round toggle set
- 12" flexible wire

Toolbox
- Wire cutters
- Flat nose or chain nose pliers

What You Need to Know

See the instructions and information outlined in Single-Strand Basics, pages 23-29, as well as the information in Earring and Dangle Basics, pages 36-40.

Tip

● Placing a small seed bead 11/0 or 13/0 between pearls can emulate the look of knotting between pearls.

Did you know?

● Bridal parties are a fun way to make jewelry for the big wedding day. Make jewelry to match dresses and help the bride choose and make her own bridal jewelry too.

Sarah Dangle Bracelet

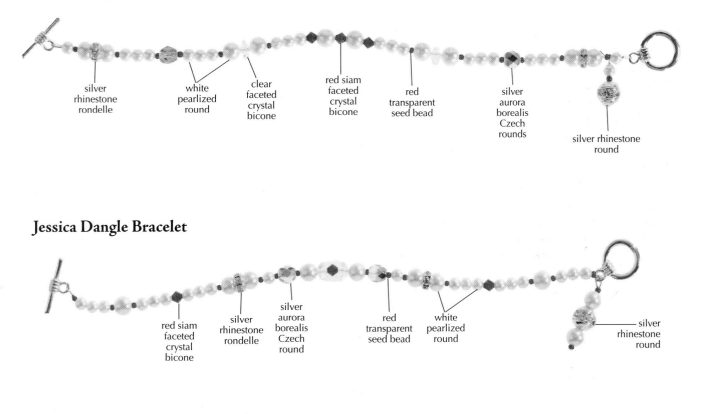

silver rhinestone rondelle

white pearlized round

clear faceted crystal bicone

red siam faceted crystal bicone

red transparent seed bead

silver aurora borealis Czech rounds

silver rhinestone round

Jessica Dangle Bracelet

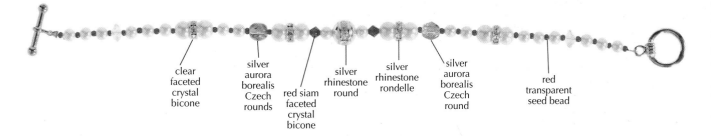

red siam faceted crystal bicone

silver rhinestone rondelle

silver aurora borealis Czech round

red transparent seed bead

white pearlized round

silver rhinestone round

Kristen Bracelet

clear faceted crystal bicone

silver aurora borealis Czech rounds

red siam faceted crystal bicone

silver rhinestone round

silver rhinestone rondelle

silver aurora borealis Czech round

red transparent seed bead

Blushing Bride Necklace

Designer: *Shannon Williams*

Finished Size: 14¾" without clasp
Where to Get It: Craft stores
Time to Complete: One weekend
How Much Will It Cost? A movie and popcorn (less than $20)

silver lined
clear seed
bead

white
pearlized
round

white
pearlized
round

clear faceted
crystal
bicone

clear faceted
crystal bicone

clear aurora
borealis faceted
crystal round

What You Need

54 white pearlized
7.5mm rounds
13 white pearlized
4mm rounds
6mm white pearlized round
40 silver-lined clear
11/0 seed beads
6 clear 4mm faceted
crystal bicones
4mm x 6mm clear
faceted crystal bicone
7mm clear aurora borealis
faceted crystal round
2 silver 3mm rounds
2 silver 2mm x 3mm
crimp beads
Silver hook-and-eye clasp set
13 sterling silver 3" headpins
19" flexible wire

Toolbox

Wire cutters
Flat nose or chain nose pliers
Round nose pliers

This is a lovely necklace for a lovely bride. What fun to design your own bridal party jewelry. It's memorable, unique and often less expensive than pre-made jewelry from your bridal salon.

What You Need to Know

See the instructions and information outlined in Single-Strand Basics, pages 23-29, as well as those in Earring and Dangle Basics, pages 36-40.

Tip

●**Do not place dangles much beyond the 6" mark each side of center on a choker or the 8" mark on an 18" or 20" necklace as the dangles can irritate skin near a collar or catch onto delicate lace. Of course, if you are wearing an off-the-shoulder gown you could place dangles throughout the necklace.**

Lilacs in Bloom Lariat Necklace

What a find in any treasure box. This lanky amethyst lariat could be a standard in any fashion wardrobe.

Designer: *Annie Hinton*

Finished Size: 36" crimp to crimp; 4" dangles each side
Where to Get It: Specialty bead shops or catalogs; craft stores
Time to Complete: One weekend
How Much Will It Cost? A movie and popcorn (less than $20)

What You Need to Know

See the instructions and information outlined in Single-Strand Basics, pages 23-29, as well as those in Findings and Closures, pages 32-35.

Tip

●Hanging two headpin beaded dangles from each end of a lariat is a clever way to finish the ends without becoming too bendable.

What You Need

108 purple transparent 6/0 seed beads
72 copper-lined clear 6/0 seed beads
35 purple transparent 5mm rounds
24 clear aurora borealis copper 5mm rounds
7mm clear aurora borealis copper round
12 copper 7mm rounds
2 gold 6mm rounds
6 gold 4mm x 3mm cylinders
10 gold rosebud 8mm rounds

4 purple transparent 10mm rounds
4 gold 2½" chains
4 gold 4" headpins
2 gold 4" eyepins
2 gold 6mm jump rings
2 gold 2mm x 3mm crimp beads
40" flexible wire

Toolbox

Wire cutters
Flat nose or chain nose pliers

purple transparent round

copper transparent seed bead

purple transparent seed bead

gold round

gold cylinder

gold jump ring

gold chain

gold rosebud round

purple transparent round

carnelain disc

eggshell opaque round

amber faceted disc

light blue opaque round

quartz crystal nugget

turquoise disc

lampwork

peridot chip

Monet's Lilies Transition Necklace

Designer: *Susan Ray*
Lampwork Artists:
  Trent and Shawn Warden

Finished Size:
49¼" without clasp
Where to Get It: From the artist
Time to Complete:
One afternoon
How Much Will It Cost?
Dinner for two ($50 to $100)

What You Need

8mm x 11mm lampwork bead
8 lampwork 5mm x 10mm beads
12 quartz 10mm x 15mm
  crystal nuggets
4 amber 5mm x 10mm discs
19 light blue opaque
  5mm rounds
8 amber 3mm x 6mm
  faceted discs
15 citrine chips
32 lapis chips
35 peridot chips
30 light blue opaque
  4mm rounds
7mm light green
  faceted crystal round
8 eggshell opaque
  5mm rounds
3 amber 3mm x 10mm
  faceted discs
4 turquoise 5mm x 6mm discs
2 salmon 5mm x 6mm discs
4 carnelian 6mm x 10mm discs
30 gold 8/0 seed beads
2 sterling silver 2mm x 3mm
  crimp beads
Sterling silver lobster claw clasp
6mm silver split ring
54" flexible wire

Toolbox

Wire cutters
Flat nose or chain nose pliers

What You Need to Know

See the instructions and information outlined in Single-Strand Basics, pages 23-29.

The painterly transition of color is masterfully reproduced in this necklace of beautiful natural stone chips, reticulated quartz and luminous lampwork beads.

Buy American

● Mass-produced lampwork beads can fracture since they are sometimes not annealed. Look closely for lopsidedness and inconsistencies. Or a "powder" interior that generally means they have not been cleaned properly. When it seems like too good of a deal, it probably is too good of a deal.

Tip

● Interested in learning more about stringing with lampwork beads? Read Susan Ray and Richard Pearce's, The Art and Soul of Glass Beads. The book details the life and work of 14 distinguished lampwork artists as well as giving you helpful tips when shopping for the perfect bead.

Toss 'em Necklace and Bracelet

You'll end up a winner with this fresh ensemble that features teal and mango combined with deep garnet chips.

Designer: *Leigh Meyer*

Necklace
Finished Size: 13" without clasp
Where to Get It: Specialty bead shops or catalogs
Time to Complete: One afternoon
How Much Will It Cost? A manicure ($20 to $50)

Bracelet
Finished Size: 6" without clasp
Where to Get It: Specialty bead shops or catalogs
Time to Complete: One hour
How Much Will It Cost? A movie and popcorn (less than $20)

What You Need to Know
For both the necklace and bracelet: See the instructions and information outlined in Single-Strand Basics, pages 23-29.

Tip
● The saying "measure twice and cut once" also applies to jewelry-making. Remember to "measure twice and crimp once."

garnet chip

malachite teal chip

Chinese carnelian mango disc

Words of Inspiration
My outstanding husband, Stephen, and I have three boys. Quincey is 4 and we have 22-month-old twins, Elias and Riley. I obviously don't have much time to dedicate to my beading, but when I'm feeling creative and need to relax, I drag out my beloved beads and go at it.
—Leigh Meyer

What You Need

Necklace
100 garnet chips*
10 malachite teal chips*
9 Chinese carnelian mango 6mm discs
2 sterling silver 2mm x 3mm crimp beads
Silver toggle set
18" flexible wire

*Available through Fire Mountain Gems

Bracelet
36 garnet chips
6 malachite chips
5 Chinese carnelian 6mm discs
2 sterling silver 2mm x 3mm crimp beads
Silver toggle set
12" flexible wire

Toolbox
Wire cutters
Flat nose or chain nose pliers

Dichroic Fiesta Double-Strand Pendant

Designer: *Sue Wilke*

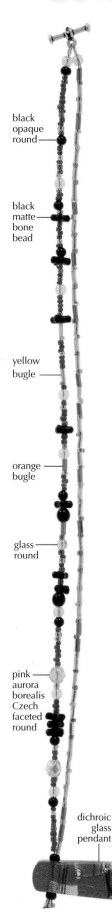

black
opaque
round

black
matte
bone
bead

yellow
bugle

orange
bugle

glass
round

pink
aurora
borealis
Czech
faceted
round

dichroic
glass
pendant

Finished Size: 23" without clasp
Where to Get It: Specialty bead shops or catalogs; from the artist; on the Web
Time to Complete: One weekend
How Much Will It Cost?
A manicure ($20 to $50)

What You Need to Know

See the instructions and information outlined in Multi-Strand Basics, pages 30-31, plus the specifics for stringing the pendant below.

Here's How to String the Pendant:

1. String both wires through the pendant and slide the pendant to the center of the wires.

2. String beads onto each wire, as with any multi-strand piece.

3. Attach the clasp, as usual.

Tips

● Bugle beads have sharp edges that can cut some types of stringing materials. Experts sometimes use clear nail polish on the edges to prevent the edges from fraying thread.

● Place a large mix of complimentary accent beads in a bowl. The beads are then strung in a random pattern. Although the necklace appears balanced upon close examination, it in fact is not symmetrical.

The alternating patterns on the strands of this necklace glitter festively, reflecting light in this fiery dichroic glass pendant.

What You Need

- 11mm x 35mm dichroic glass rectangle pendant
- 18 clear 4mm glass rounds
- 17 black opaque 3mm rounds
- 3 black opaque 5mm rounds
- 19 black matte 3mm x 7mm bones
- 7 pink aurora borealis Czech 6mm faceted rounds
- 85 yellow transparent 11/0 seed beads
- 28 Siam red transparent 11/0 seed beads
- 6 red matte 11/0 seed beads
- 15 red opaque 11/0 seed beads
- 96 red-orange transparent 11/0 seed beads
- 68 orange transparent 11/0 seed beads
- 17 orange opaque 11/0 seed beads
- 17 orange-and-pink aurora borealis 11/0 seed beads
- 24 fuchsia rainbow 11/0 seed beads
- 4 fuchsia aurora borealis 11/0 seed beads
- 19 yellow 1.5mm x 5mm bugle beads
- 19 orange 1.5mm x 5mm bugle beads
- 35 light yellow 1.5mm x 5mm bugle beads
- 4 sterling silver 2mm x 3mm crimp beads
- Sterling silver toggle set
- 2 27" lengths flexible wire

Toolbox

Wire cutters
Flat nose or chain nose pliers

Barnyard Tuxedo Three-Strand Necklace

Designer: *Sue Wilke*
Lampwork Artist: *Jill Shank*

Finished Size: 18", 20", 22" without clasp
Where to Get It: From the artist
Time to Complete: One afternoon
How Much Will It Cost? A manicure
($20 to $50)

What You Need
Rooster lampwork bead
Black sheep lampwork bead
White sheep lampwork bead
Black-and-white cow lampwork bead
Pink pig lampwork bead
Black horse lampwork bead
808 black shiny 13/0 seed beads
52 brown matte 11/0 seed beads
18 black shiny 6/0 seed beads
27 black 5mm rounds
6 sterling silver 2mm x 3mm
   crimp beads
Silver three-strand clasp set
22" length flexible wire
24" length flexible wire
26" length flexible wire

Toolbox
Wire cutters
Flat nose or chain nose pliers

These whimsical barnyard creatures never looked so formal, as marching along this three-strand necklace.

What You Need to Know

See the instructions and information outlined in Multi-Strand Basics, pages 30-31.

lampwork rooster

black
round

black
lampwork
sheep

white
lampwork
sheep

black shiny
seed bead

lampwork
cow

lampwork
pig

lampwork
horse

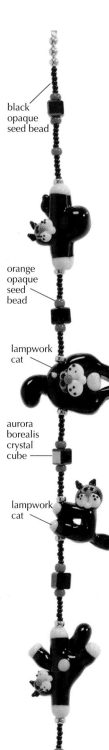

black
opaque
seed bead

orange
opaque
seed
bead

lampwork
cat

aurora
borealis
crystal
cube

lampwork
cat

lampwork
cat pendant

Cat's Meow Necklace

Designer: *Susan Ray*
Lampwork Artist:
Amy Caswell

Finished Size:
22½" without clasp
Where to Get It: From the artist
Time to Complete: One weekend
How Much Will It Cost?
One-way ticket to London
(more than $100)

What You Need
8 cat lampwork beads
Cat lampwork pendant
6 sterling silver 3mm rounds*
18 sterling silver 4mm spacers
126 black opaque
   11/0 seed beads
21 orange/red opaque
   6/0 seed beads
10 black aurora borealis
   6mm crystal cubes**
2 sterling silver 2mm x 3mm
   crimp beads
Sterling silver spring-ring clasp
27" flexible wire
*Available through Westrim
**Available through Halcraft

Toolbox
Wire cutters
Flat nose or chain nose pliers

What You Need to Know
See the instructions and
information outlined in Single-
Strand Basics, pages 23-29.

Check out these classy cats performing hijinks on a high wire.

Words of Inspiration
Amy Caswell likes the novelty of lampwork:
*"I'd rather wear something distinctive and one-of-a-kind. The
worth of a good glass bead can be both seen and felt."*

Breast Cancer Awareness Bracelet and American Heart Association Necklace

With the pink ribbon for breast cancer and heart charm for heart disease, the awareness symbols raise our consciousness and that of those who see this bracelet or necklace worn.

Designers: *Carol Coyle and Susan Ray*

Breast Cancer Awareness* Crystal-and-Silver Bracelet

Designer: Carol Coyle
Finished Size: 6¾" without clasp
Where to Get It: Specialty bead shop or catalogs; craft stores
Time to Complete: One weekend
How Much Will It Cost?
A manicure ($20 to $50)

American Heart Association* Necklace

Designer: Susan Ray
Finished Size: 17" without clasp
Where to Get It: Specialty bead shop or catalogs; craft stores
Time to Complete: One weekend
How Much Will It Cost?
A manicure ($20 to $50)
*See resources for more information on these charitable organizations, page 143.

What You Need to Know

For the bracelet: See the instructions and information outlined in Single-Strand Basics, pages 23-29.

For the necklace: See the instructions and information outlined in Multi-Strand Basics, pages 30-31.

What You Need

Bracelet
8 rose 4mm bicones
4 rose 5mm bicones
10 crystal Rondelles
28 silver-lined clear
    11/0 seed beads
8 silver 4mm corrugated beads
5.5mm alphabet blocks,
    as follows: 2 hearts, 1 ribbon
2 sterling silver 2mm x 3mm
    crimp beads
Sterling silver toggle set
12" flexible wire

Necklace
154 silver 8/0 seed beads
601 magenta 11/0 seed beads
40 white pearl 5mm glass rounds
Silver heart pendant
Silver toggle set
6 sterling silver 2mm x 3mm
    crimp beads
6mm silver jump ring
Three 21" lengths of flexible wire

Toolbox
Wire cutters
Flat nose or chain nose pliers

silver corrugated bead

rose bicone

crystal bicone

ribbon alphabet block

Appendices

Beads abound. Study the shapes, facets and finishes. Many beads are priced based on the composition of the bead, origin and quality. Just as with diamonds, beads can be rated by their color, transparency, number of facets and the like. Make a note of the country of origin. It is fun to use beads from faraway places. Craft stores have large varieties of beads if you do not have a local bead shop in your area. Lampwork is more difficult to find in many areas and can be more expensive than the copies craft stores offer. Handmade lampwork is unique and often only one of a kind is available. You will easily find lampwork online at auctions and at many artists' own Web sites. Use your favorite search engine to hunt for "lampwork" or "glass beads." Study bead magazines. Many artists and distributors advertise in *Bead and Button*, *Beadwork*, *Lapidary Journal* and *Bead Style*, as well as other bead magazines.

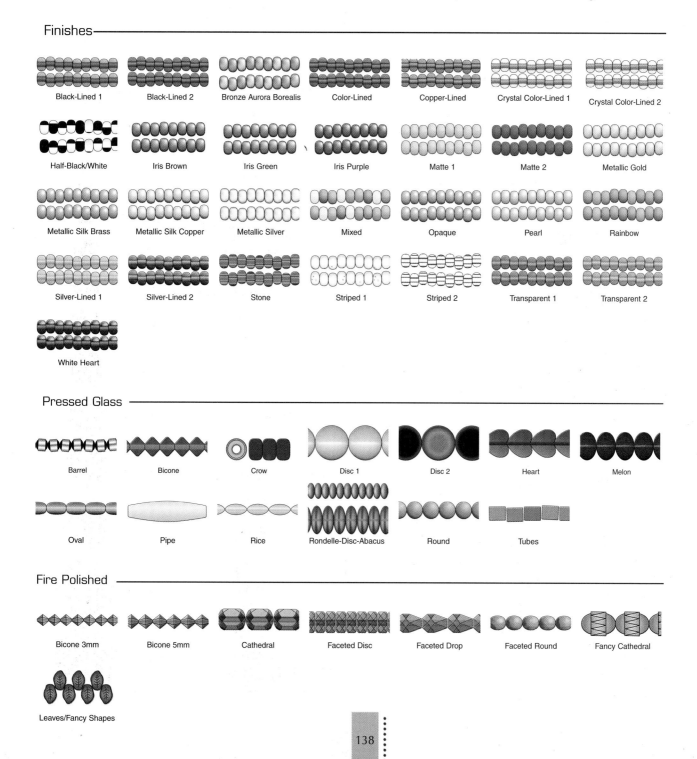

Finishes

Black-Lined 1 · Black-Lined 2 · Bronze Aurora Borealis · Color-Lined · Copper-Lined · Crystal Color-Lined 1 · Crystal Color-Lined 2

Half-Black/White · Iris Brown · Iris Green · Iris Purple · Matte 1 · Matte 2 · Metallic Gold

Metallic Silk Brass · Metallic Silk Copper · Metallic Silver · Mixed · Opaque · Pearl · Rainbow

Silver-Lined 1 · Silver-Lined 2 · Stone · Striped 1 · Striped 2 · Transparent 1 · Transparent 2

White Heart

Pressed Glass

Barrel · Bicone · Crow · Disc 1 · Disc 2 · Heart · Melon

Oval · Pipe · Rice · Rondelle-Disc-Abacus · Round · Tubes

Fire Polished

Bicone 3mm · Bicone 5mm · Cathedral · Faceted Disc · Faceted Drop · Faceted Round · Fancy Cathedral

Leaves/Fancy Shapes

Size & Shape Samples

11/0 Three-Cut	11/0 Rocaille	11/0 True-cut	13/0 Charlotte	6/0 Rocaille	8/0 Rocaille	Miyuki Delica Bead

Size #1 Super Twisted	Size #2 Bugle Bead	Size #20 Bugle Bead	Size #3 Bugle Bead	Size #3 Twisted Bugle Bead	Size #30 Twisted Bugle Bead	Size #5 Bugle Bead

Additional Bead Shapes

Abacus	Barrel	Chip Beads	Cylinder	Heishe	Oval	Square

Bead Sizes

Metric is the name of the game when it comes to beads. Beads come from all over the world and since the metric system is used elsewhere, beads are measured in millimeters more often than not. If you never were a fan of metric, here are simple charts to help you make the transistion. Be sure to keep your chart handy when buying beads online. Photos can often distort the size of a bead. Be sure to read the fine print when purchasing beads online or in catalogs.

How many beads make a 16" strand?

Approximately:
- 2mm = 203 beads
- 3mm = 136 beads
- 4mm = 100 beads
- 6mm = 67 beads
- 8mm = 50 beads
- 10mm = 41 beads
- 12mm = 34 beads

Bugle Bead Sizes

1 2 3 5

Millimeter/ Inch Gauge

mm inches

Size

| 7/0 |
| 8/0 |
| 9/0 |
| 10/0 |
| 11/0 |
| 12/0 |
| 14/0 |
| 16/0 |
| 20/0 |

Square MM Sizes

- 3x3mm ■
- 4x4mm ■
- 5x5mm ■

Seed Beads Per Inch

Use these approximate counts of seed beads per inch to help plan your own designs

Bead Size	Beads per inch
11/0	20
8/0	12
5/0	7

Oval Bead Sizes in Millimeters

- 6 x 4
- 7 x 5
- 8 x 6
- 10 x 8
- 12 x 10
- 14 x 10
- 16 x 12

Round Bead Sizes in Millimeters

- 2 mm
- 3 mm
- 4 mm
- 5 mm
- 6 mm
- 7 mm
- 8 mm
- 9 mm
- 10 mm
- 11 mm
- 12 mm
- 14 mm
- 16 mm
- 18 mm

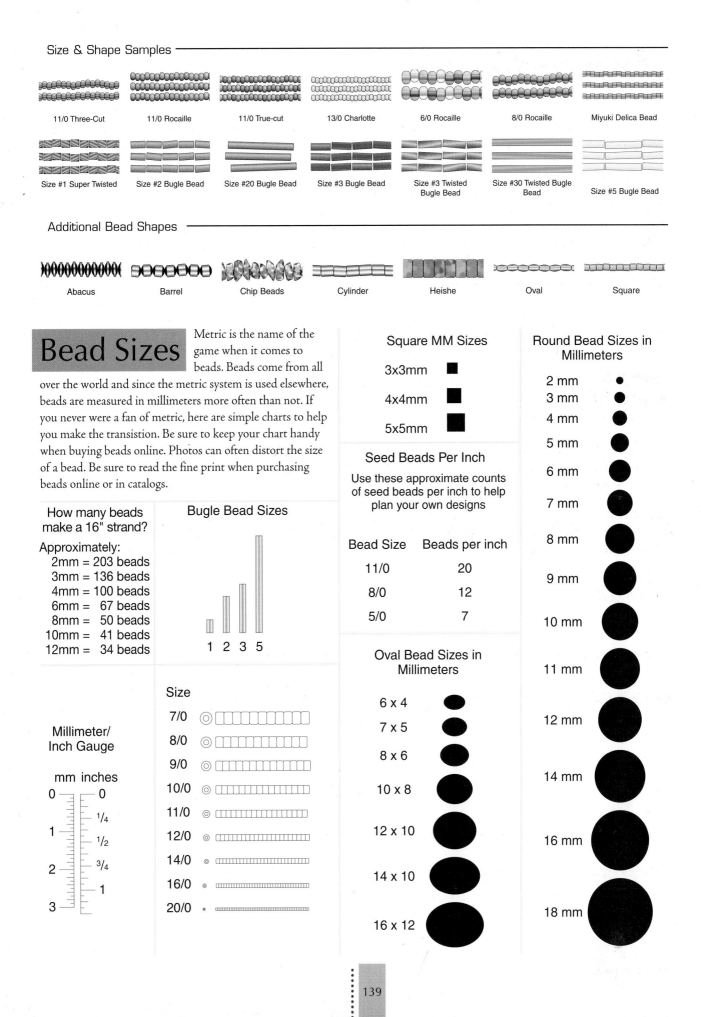

139

Findings

Jewelry findings are available at craft and bead stores. With some luck, you can find wonderful vintage findings at thrift and resale shops.

Crimps are available in many weights and materials. A cardinal rule: Don't skimp on crimps. Use crimp beads in sterling in at least half-hard silver and heavier gauge wire. Available from bead stores and bead distributors, these crimps are more expensive but worth every penny. Quality crimps will ensure you enjoy your new beaded jewelry for years to come. We recommend 2mm x 3mm and 2mm x 2mm half-hard sterling silver crimps and heavier gauge wire for the majority of your work.

Try to add a sterling or gold plate 2mm or 3mm ball to the end of your stringing right before your crimp bead. The additional ball helps support the wear and tear each crimp bead takes. String the flexible wire back through the crimp bead, ball and at least 1" of beads before cutting away the short end.

Ear wires are available in many styles. Try on ear wires before buying too many. Different styles of ear wires fit the ear differently. Surgical steel and sterling are best for sensitive ears.

Clasps are also available in many new styles. If you prefer toggles, be sure that the bar-end is larger than the loop end. This will help ensure that the toggle stays in place when you wear your jewelry. Make sure the first few beads nearest the bar-end will slip comfortably through the loop end, so you won't be able to use the toggle closure without a struggle.

Create Your Own Jump Rings

1. Coil a length of 18- to 22-gauge wire around a mandrel by hand or by using other wire coiling tools available in craft stores, online or through specialty bead shops.

2. Use wire cutters to cut a complete link from the coil.

3. Close each link tightly when connecting them together or to other portions of a piece you are working on.

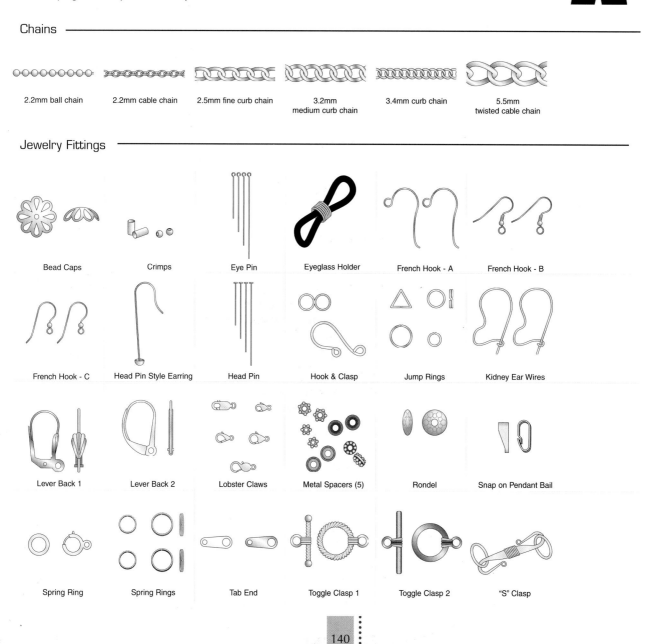

Chains

2.2mm ball chain	2.2mm cable chain	2.5mm fine curb chain	3.2mm medium curb chain	3.4mm curb chain	5.5mm twisted cable chain

Jewelry Fittings

Bead Caps   Crimps   Eye Pin   Eyeglass Holder   French Hook - A   French Hook - B

French Hook - C   Head Pin Style Earring   Head Pin   Hook & Clasp   Jump Rings   Kidney Ear Wires

Lever Back 1   Lever Back 2   Lobster Claws   Metal Spacers (5)   Rondel   Snap on Pendant Bail

Spring Ring   Spring Rings   Tab End   Toggle Clasp 1   Toggle Clasp 2   "S" Clasp

Jewelry Lengths

How many beads do you need? A simple way to figure out how many beads your necklace will require is to take a sampling of the beads you are planning to use and line them up on your bead board. Cover a 4" length. Count the number of beads that will be required to cover this 4". Determine the desired finished length and divide by 4. Use this number to multiply by the number of beads in your 4" sample.

This will give you the number of beads in your finished necklace. Example: If it takes 12 beads to fill the 4" length and you want your finished necklace to be 20", divide 20" by 4" (equals 5) and then multiply 12 by 5 for an outcome of 60 beads needed to complete your piece.

Use your bead board! The board offers accurate measurements for multiple necklaces and it allows you to change bead order or even change the type of beads used without disturbing your design work.

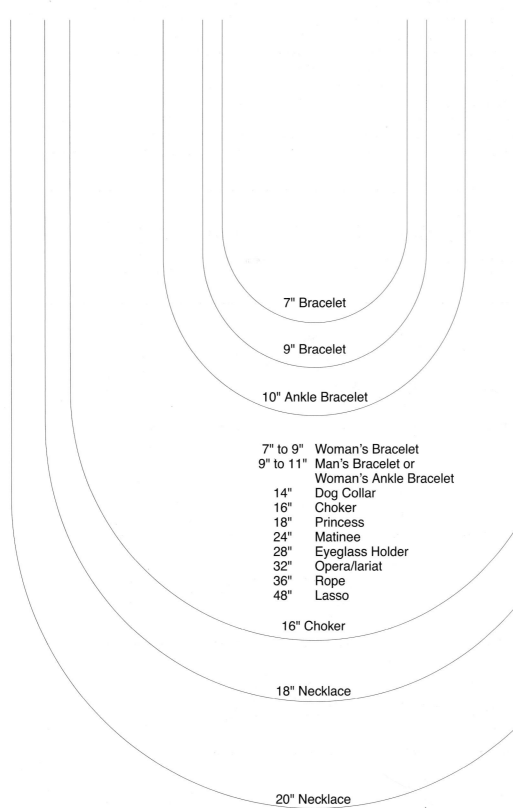

7" Bracelet

9" Bracelet

10" Ankle Bracelet

7" to 9"	Woman's Bracelet
9" to 11"	Man's Bracelet or Woman's Ankle Bracelet
14"	Dog Collar
16"	Choker
18"	Princess
24"	Matinee
28"	Eyeglass Holder
32"	Opera/lariat
36"	Rope
48"	Lasso

16" Choker

18" Necklace

20" Necklace

Jewelry Designers

Carol Coyle
Carol's Creations
215 Tyler St.
Cascade, IA 52033
(563) 852-3451
e-mail: zipee@netins.net

Jan Harris
Pangea Art on Main—
   The Bead Bar
109 N. Main St.
Galena, IL 61036
(815) 777-4080
e-mail: pangeagalena@msn.com
www.pangeagallery.com

Jeanne Holland
Vintaj
704 Park Ave.
Galena, IL 61036
(815) 541-5558
e-mail: jeanne@karmul.com
www.vintaj.com

Jessica Italia
The Bead Bar
109 N. Main St.
Galena, IL 61036
(815) 777-4080
e-mail: galenabeadbar@msn.com
www.galenabeadbar.com

Alyson Leahy
Art By Al
137 W. Main St.
Shullsburg, WI 53586
e-mail: allycat0586@hotmail.com

Wendy Mullane
Vintaj
704 Park Ave.
Galena, IL 61036
(815) 541-0219
e-mail: WMullane@karmul.com
www.vintaj.com

Susan Ray
18098 Fulton Road
Maquoketa, IA 52060
(563) 652-3307
e-mail: raysa524@aol.com
eBay ID: galenabeadtrader

Claire Russ
Galena, Ill.
e-mail: cjruss@galenalink.com

Shannon Williams
2580 Windy Lane
Galena, IL 61036
e-mail: embroidery@bhawk.net

Sue Wilke
15955 Lore Mound Road
Dubuque, IA 52002
(563) 583-1083

Linda Zsevc
P.O. Box 6061-362
Sherman Oaks, CA 91413
(818) 989-1769
e-mail: IMLMZ@hotmail.com

Lampwork Artist Directory

Iris Buchholtz
Iris Glass Art
3333 Par Drive
Oceanside, CA 92056
(760) 721-7355
e-mail: Irisglassart@cox.net
www.IrisGlassArt.com

Amy Caswell
Caswell Glass Studio
173 S. Vento Park Road
Newbury Park, CA 91320
(805) 499-0707
e-mail: amy@caswellstudios.com
www.caswellstudios.com

Leigh Funk
Funky Beads
2708 E. 46th St.
Davenport, IA 52807
e-mail: lfunk@tranquility.net

Gary Haun
1650 Little Fishtrap Road
Lawrenceburg, TN 38464
(931) 722-9164
e-mail: garyh@netease.net

**Rebecca and
David Jurgens**
L and S Arts
e-mail: landsart1@aol.com
eBay ID: landsart
www.landsart.com

Tamara Knight
Knight Beads
32 Windwood Drive
Aurora, IL 60506
e-mail: knightbeads@aol.com
eBay ID: Knightbeads

Karen Leonardo
Just Leonardo
362 Hood School Road
Indiana, PA 15701
(724) 357-8709
e-mail: justleo7@ptdprolog.net
eBay ID: justleonardo
www.justleonardo.com

Roberta Ogborn
e-mail: Obobbio@msn.com
eBay ID: trappedinabead

Deb Roesly
Little Crow Glass Art
Howard City, MI 49329
e-mail: LittlecrowOriginals
   @hotmail.com
www.littlecrowglassart.com

Jill Shank
Bluebird Bead Farm
9998 E. 460 Road
Claremore, OK 74017
(918) 342-2101
e-mail: jill@bluebirdbeads.com
www.bluebirdbeads.com

Trent and Shawn Warden
Xbead
P.O. Box 2335
Mesilla Park, NM 88047
(505) 527-5434
e-mail: xbead@zianet.com
eBay ID: Xbead

Contributors

Brittany Berndtson
Galena, Illinois

Susan Brusch
Galena, Illinois

Brenda Duhme
Maquoketa, Iowa

Julie Ann Duhme
Washington, DC

Linda Duhme
Maquoketa, Iowa

Sol Hernandez
Galena, Illinois

Annie Hinton
Galena, Illinois

Darien Kaiser
East Dubuque, Illinois

Krysti Kehl
Dubuque, Iowa

Kelly Laugesen
Dubuque, Iowa

Amber Malone
Ames, Iowa

Elizabeth Malone
Ames, Iowa

Loralee Malone
Ames, Iowa

Leigh Meyer
Galena, Illinois

Linda Duhme Olson
Arlington Heights, Illinois

Laureen Schwenker
Maquoketa, Iowa

Jill Schwenker
Maquoketa, Iowa

Mary Beth Sprengelmeyer
East Dubuque, Illinois

Christen Stretch
Galena, Illinois

Resources

American Cancer Society

Make a general contribution or a fast, secure memorial contribution to celebrate the memory of someone who has died from cancer. Express special appreciation year-round by making a gift in honor of the special occasions in your loved one's lives—holidays, anniversaries, graduation, birthdays, and more. To donate either call (800) ACS-2345 or simply download the form from the Web site (www.cancer.org), print it and mail the completed donor form with your check to:

American Cancer Society
ATTN: Web
  P.O. Box 102454
  Atlanta, GA 30368-2454

American Heart Association

A memorial donation will honor the memory of a loved one. A tribute will celebrate a friend or family member's accomplishment. These and general donations are vitally important, as they help fund research and education programs that fight heart disease and stroke. For donation questions or assistance, call (800) 242-8721 or visit the Web site at www.americanheart.org.

Blue Moon Beads,
A Creativity Inc. Company

7855 Hayvenhurst Ave.
Van Nuys, CA 91406
(800) 377-6715
www.bluemoonbeads.com

Crystal Cottage Studio

Shelly Penko
3664 Ridgeland Road
West Bloomfield, MI 48323
(248) 855-2989
e-mail: shelly@crystalcottagestudio.com or penko@crystalcottagestudio.com
www.crystalcottagestudio.com
eBay user ID: crystalcottage
Features beautiful stones and high-quality and unusual gem beads primarily as an eBay-based business, owned and operated by husband and wife team Andrew and Shelly Penko. The inventory changes almost monthly. Requests for special stones in various shapes and sizes are welcomed, as are questions via e-mail.

Fire Mountain Gems

1 Fire Mountain Way
Grants Pass, OR 97526
(800) 423-2319
e-mail: questions@firemtn.com
www.firemountaingems.com
Publishes comprehensive bead and supply catalog each year, plus supplementary catalogs, available on the company's Web site.

FPC Corporation

355 Hollow Hill Drive
Wauconda, IL 60084
(847) 487-4583
fax: (847) 487-0174
e-mail: glueguns@aol.com
www.surebonder.com
Manufactures glue guns; glue; adhesives; staple guns; staples; floral tools; home tools for women; bead kits; faux wax kits and sticks; and home décor kits.

Gutermann of America

8227 Arrowridge Blvd.
Charlotte, NC 28273
(704) 525-7068
e-mail: info@gutermann-us.com
Manufactures fabric and quilting and needlecraft supplies.

Halcraft USA Inc.

Cliff Wallach
60 S. Macquesten Parkway
Mt. Vernon, NY 10550
(212) 376-1580
e-mail: clifford@halcraft.com
Offers art materials; beads and bead kits; children's activity kits; craft suppliers; holiday/seasonal; home decorating; jewelry findings and supplies; party supplies; rubber stamps; stationary; transfers/decals; and wedding accessories.

Judikins, Inc.

Judi Watanabe
17803 S. Harvard Blvd.
Gardena, CA 90248
(310) 515-1115
e-mail: customerservice@judikins.com
www.judikins.com

Rio Grande

7500 Bluewater Road, NW
Albuquerque, NM 87121
(800) 545-6566
e-mail: info@riogrande.com
www.riogrande.com
Offers extensive selection of gems, findings and bead products shown actual size in the company's catalog, which can be ordered on the Web site.

Vintaj/Karmul Studios

704 Park Ave.
Galena, IL 61036
e-mail: buy@karmul.com
www.vintaj.com
Original art jewelry designed using an innovative "brass encased glass" settings concept developed by Wendy Mullane and Jeanne Holland.

Westrim Crafts,
A Creativity Inc. Company

7855 Hayvenhurst Ave.
Van Nuys, CA 91406
(800) 727-2727
www.westrimcrafts.com
Manufactures beads and bead kits; children's activity kits; craft supplies; jewelry findings and supplies; metal and wire craft; scrapbooks; soapmaking; and stickers.

About the Authors

Susan Ray

Susan Ray has more than 20 years of experience in the craft industry as author, buyer and merchandise manager, vice president of product, and in Web site development. The strength of Susan's entrepreneurial spirit has attracted many companies to utilize her expertise in formulating new store concepts. She was co-founder of an award-winning computer exploration facility, which received a ComputerWorld Smithsonian Award for heroic innovation of technology. She currently serves as founder of Bubbles, Bangles and Beads, a bead emporium, in Galena, Ill. She is co-author of *The Art and Soul of Glass Beads* (KP Books, 2003) and her craft and interior designs have been featured in numerous national publications. She resides in the beautiful tourist town of Galena, Ill., with her son, Eric.

Sue Wilke

Sue Wilke has an art education degree from Luther College in Decorah, Iowa, and has taught art in public schools. Sue has been in business for more than 20 years, with much experience in retail merchandising, buying, store planning and design. She is the creator and proprietor of Ink and Stamp with Sue, a unique store in Galena, Ill., that features rubber-stamping, scrapbooking and a wide array of supplies and embellishments for all paper and ink arts. Sue has taught classes and workshops on a large variety of techniques and materials. Sue's knack for color crosses the boundaries of all her hobbies from gardening and decorating to needlework, beading and knitting. Sue resides in the historic river town of Dubuque, Iowa, with her spaniel, Bailey.

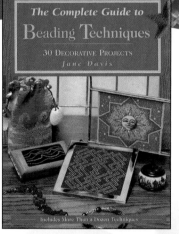